REAL SIMPLE | best recipes

easy, delicious meals

RECIPES EDITED BY
LYGEIA GRACE AND KATE MERKER

REAL SIMPLE  Time Inc.
HOME ENTERTAINMENT

WHAT MAKES a recipe memorable? Is it:

(a) The ingredients.

(b) The ingenuity with which the ingredients are combined.

(c) The final product.

(d) The context: how you feel when you're making or eating it, the people you're sharing it with.

(e) All of the above.

THE ANSWER IS (E), of course, with one important caveat: that you're also able to say, "Wow, that was easy!" as you sit down to eat. Combine all these elements and you have a recipe you'll remember, one that, over time, will become dog-eared and stained with the makings of great meals gone by.

AT REAL SIMPLE, we have fought for 10 years against the idea that a satisfying meal requires a lot of labor up front, either in searching for exotic ingredients or in slaving away in the kitchen. We're also committed to coming up with recipes that support a healthy diet—using antioxidant-rich vegetables, for example, and no more fats and oils than necessary—without compromising deliciousness. The bottom line: Our food editors know that there's nothing more satisfying—or sensible, for that matter—than seasonal ingredients prepared simply, so that the flavors, and not the labor involved, shine through.

WITH THIS STANDARD IN MIND, we publish memorable recipes in *Real Simple* magazine every single month. The labor comes in trying to decide which of them *not* to include in a cookbook like this one. What you have in your hands is an edited collection of some of our most memorable recipes. We hope they become yours as well.

Kristin van Ogtrop

KRISTIN VAN OGTROP
Managing Editor, *Real Simple*

contents

Rosemary Pecans (recipe, page 15).

appetizers

Think of an appetizer as the opening act for dinner—something to keep your hungry guests occupied and allow you time to give the headliner (that would be the main course) one last wardrobe check. Let these tasty snacks, from three-ingredient pigs in a blanket to elegant crostini with chickpeas and mint, whet your audience's appetite for what's to come. They're almost as effortless as your standby chips and salsa but so impressive, they might just steal the show.

RECIPE KEY
🕐 30 MINUTES OR LESS
♥ HEART-HEALTHY
🍲 ONE POT
🍄 VEGETARIAN
✖ NO-COOK
🧸 KID-FRIENDLY
❄ FREEZABLE

Parmesan twists

HANDS-ON TIME: 15 MINUTES |
TOTAL TIME: 30 MINUTES | MAKES 24

  1 17.3-ounce package frozen puff pastry, thawed
  1 large egg, lightly beaten
1½ cups grated Parmesan (6 ounces)
  1 tablespoon poppy or sesame seeds (optional)

> Heat oven to 400° F. Cut the puff pastry length-wise into 24 strips and transfer to 2 baking sheets.

> Brush each strip with the egg and sprinkle with the Parmesan and poppy seeds, if using. Twist the strips and bake until puffed and golden brown, 12 to 15 minutes. Serve warm or at room temperature.

TIP
These twists are great
with a variety of toppings.
Instead of poppy seeds,
try fennel or cumin seeds
or a dried spice, like
paprika or cayenne.

pears with blue cheese and prosciutto

HANDS-ON TIME: 10 MINUTES |
TOTAL TIME: 10 MINUTES | SERVES 8

2 pears (such as Bosc or Bartlett), each cut into 8 wedges
2 teaspoons fresh lemon juice
1 cup arugula
3 ounces blue cheese, cut into small pieces
6 ounces thinly sliced prosciutto, cut in half lengthwise

> In a large bowl, toss the pears and lemon juice.

> Layer a slice of pear, an arugula leaf, and a piece of cheese on a piece of prosciutto and roll up.

TIP
Are pears out of season?
Prosciutto and blue cheese
deliciously complement
many fruits, including juicy
peaches and cantaloupe
and honeydew melons.

provolone and roasted red pepper crisps

HANDS-ON TIME: 10 MINUTES |
TOTAL TIME: 20 MINUTES | SERVES 8

2 pitas, each split into 2 rounds
4 tablespoons olive oil
1 teaspoon paprika
½ teaspoon dried oregano
 Kosher salt
1 16-ounce jar roasted red peppers,
 drained and cut into strips
1 clove garlic, thinly sliced
1 teaspoon fresh lemon juice
1 cup grated provolone

> Heat broiler. Arrange the pita halves cut-side up on a broilerproof baking sheet. Brush with 2 table-spoons of the oil and sprinkle with the paprika, oregano, and ¼ teaspoon salt. Broil until crisp, 2 to 3 minutes; set aside.

> Heat the remaining 2 tablespoons of oil in a large skillet. Add the peppers, garlic, and ¼ teaspoon salt. Cook until the peppers are hot and fragrant, 2 to 3 minutes. Stir in the lemon juice.

> Top the pita halves with the pepper mixture and sprinkle with the provolone. Broil until the provolone melts, 2 to 3 minutes. Cut into pieces before serving.

easy samosas

HANDS-ON TIME: 25 MINUTES |
TOTAL TIME: 55 MINUTES | MAKES 12

1 tablespoon olive oil

1 medium onion, chopped

1½ teaspoons curry powder

Kosher salt and black pepper

2 cups store-bought refrigerated or frozen mashed potatoes, thawed (about 16 ounces)

1 10-ounce package frozen peas, thawed

1 15-ounce package refrigerated piecrusts

1 jar mango chutney (optional)

> Heat oven to 375° F. Heat the oil in a large saucepan over medium heat. Add the onion and cook, stirring occasionally, until soft and golden brown, 10 to 12 minutes. Add the curry powder, ¾ teaspoon salt, and ½ teaspoon pepper and cook, stirring, until fragrant, about 1 minute. Stir in the potatoes and peas.

> Unroll the piecrusts and cut each into 6 triangles. Place a heaping tablespoon of the potato mixture in the center of each piece. Gather the corners of the dough and pinch to form a point. Pinch the seams to seal. Transfer to a baking sheet.

> Bake the samosas until golden, 22 to 25 minutes. Serve with the mango chutney, if using.

beef cocktail sandwiches with parsley butter

HANDS-ON TIME: 10 MINUTES |
TOTAL TIME: 10 MINUTES | SERVES 8

½ cup (1 stick) butter, at room temperature
¼ cup finely chopped fresh flat-leaf parsley
   Kosher salt and black pepper
 1 baguette
½ pound sliced deli roast beef

> In a small bowl, combine the butter, parsley, and ¼ teaspoon each salt and pepper.

> Slice the baguette in half horizontally. Spread the butter on both sides of the bread. Layer the roast beef on the bottom half and sandwich with the top half. Cut crosswise into 1-inch pieces.

TIP
For a subtle boost of flavor, mix a clove of finely chopped garlic into the butter before spreading on the bread.

smoked salmon and horseradish cream with potato chips

HANDS-ON TIME: 5 MINUTES |
TOTAL TIME: 5 MINUTES | SERVES 8

8 ounces cream cheese, at room temperature
2 tablespoons prepared horseradish
2 tablespoons heavy cream
1 pound thinly sliced smoked salmon
1 5-ounce package potato chips

> In a small bowl, combine the cream cheese, horseradish, and heavy cream, stirring until smooth. Serve with the salmon and potato chips.

TIP
Thick-cut potato chips are excellent alternatives to crackers. Not only do they complement silky smoked salmon but they're also nice with soft cheeses, such as goat cheese and ricotta.

chickpea and mint crostini

HANDS-ON TIME: 10 MINUTES |
TOTAL TIME: 10 MINUTES | SERVES 8

1 15.5-ounce can chickpeas, rinsed
½ cup pomegranate seeds (from 1 small pomegranate)
¼ cup fresh mint, chopped
2 scallions, chopped
2 tablespoons extra-virgin olive oil
 Kosher salt and black pepper
1 small baguette, thinly sliced and toasted

> In a medium bowl, combine the chickpeas, pome-
granate seeds, mint, scallions, oil, ¾ teaspoon
salt, and ¼ teaspoon pepper. Serve with the bread.

TIP
This crostini topping is also
delicious tossed in a mixed
green or spinach salad.

rosemary pecans

HANDS-ON TIME: 10 MINUTES |
TOTAL TIME: 20 MINUTES | SERVES 8

2 tablespoons butter
1 teaspoon sugar
⅛ teaspoon cayenne pepper
  Kosher salt
2 cups pecan halves
2 teaspoons chopped fresh rosemary

> Heat oven to 375° F. Melt the butter in a medium skillet over medium heat. Stir in the sugar, cayenne pepper, and ½ teaspoon salt. Add the pecans and toss to coat.

> Transfer the pecans to a rimmed baking sheet and arrange in a single layer. Bake, stirring occasionally, until toasted, 10 to 12 minutes.

> Add the rosemary and toss to combine. Serve warm or at room temperature.

goat cheese bruschetta

HANDS-ON TIME: 10 MINUTES |
TOTAL TIME: 10 MINUTES | SERVES 8

½ cup extra-virgin olive oil
2 tablespoons fresh lemon juice
2 tablespoons balsamic vinegar
1 teaspoon honey
  Kosher salt and black pepper
1 small shallot, finely chopped
2 tablespoons chopped fresh herbs (such as dill,
  parsley, chives, and basil)
8 thick slices country bread, toasted
2 4-ounce packages soft goat cheese

> In a medium bowl, whisk together the oil,
lemon juice, vinegar, honey, ½ teaspoon salt, and
¼ teaspoon pepper. Stir in the shallot and herbs.

> Drizzle half the vinaigrette over the bread,
spread with the goat cheese, and drizzle with the
remaining vinaigrette.

TIP
In the summer, try
grilling—instead of
toasting—the bread.

fancy pigs in a blanket

HANDS-ON TIME: 10 MINUTES |
TOTAL TIME: 30 MINUTES | SERVES 8

1 12-ounce package fully cooked chicken sausage links
1 8-ounce sheet frozen puff pastry, thawed
⅓ cup whole-grain mustard

> Heat oven to 400° F. Cut the sausages in quarters lengthwise, then in half crosswise. Cut the puff pastry into strips 3 inches long and 1 inch wide.

> Roll the sausage pieces in the pastry strips and transfer to a parchment-lined baking sheet. Bake until puffed and golden brown, 15 to 20 minutes. Serve with the mustard for dipping.

TIP
Many supermarkets sell chicken sausages in a variety of flavors. Try this crowd-pleasing recipe using apple and roasted-garlic versions.

Butternut Squash Soup (recipe, page 31).

soups

For a humble dish, soup sure can ladle on the pressure. After all, it's supposed to take all day to prepare, cure the common cold, and sometimes even teach kids the alphabet. Relax. The following recipes—including a summery, no-cook gazpacho, an elegant seafood stew, and a new take on chicken soup— will give you plenty of stock options that will please even the pickiest of eaters. Plus, they're a cinch to prepare. You and your family will be bowled over.

RECIPE KEY

- 🕐 30 MINUTES OR LESS
- ♥ HEART-HEALTHY
- 🍲 ONE POT
- 🌱 VEGETARIAN
- ✳ NO-COOK
- 🧸 KID-FRIENDLY
- ❄ FREEZABLE

smoky corn chowder

HANDS-ON TIME: 25 MINUTES | TOTAL TIME: 45 MINUTES | SERVES 6

8 ounces sliced bacon, cut into ½-inch pieces

1 large sweet onion, chopped

2 cloves garlic, finely chopped

½ teaspoon smoked paprika

¼ teaspoon crushed red pepper

2 10-ounce packages frozen corn

3 cups low-sodium chicken or vegetable broth

1 cup half-and-half

Kosher salt and black pepper

4 scallions, thinly sliced on the diagonal

1 baguette, sliced and toasted (optional)

> Cook the bacon in a large saucepan or Dutch oven over medium heat until crisp, 6 to 8 minutes. Transfer to a paper towel–lined plate.

> Spoon off and discard all but 2 tablespoons of the drippings and return the pan to medium heat. Add the onion and cook, stirring occasionally, until soft, 5 to 7 minutes. Add the garlic, paprika, and red pepper and cook, stirring, for 2 minutes.

> Stir in the corn, broth, and half-and-half and bring to a boil. Reduce heat and simmer for 15 minutes. Transfer half the soup to a blender and puree until smooth. Return to the pot and stir in ½ teaspoon each salt and pepper.

> Divide the soup among bowls and top with the scallions and bacon. Serve with the bread, if using.

winter lentil soup

HANDS-ON TIME: 20 MINUTES | TOTAL TIME: 1 HOUR | SERVES 6

1 tablespoon olive oil

4 leeks (white and light green parts), cut into ¼-inch-thick half-moons

1 28-ounce can whole tomatoes, drained

2 sweet potatoes, peeled and cut into ½-inch pieces

1 bunch kale, thick stems removed and leaves cut into ½-inch-wide strips

½ cup brown lentils

1 tablespoon fresh thyme

Kosher salt and black pepper

¼ cup grated Parmesan (1 ounce; optional)

> Heat the oil in a large saucepan or Dutch oven over medium heat. Add the leeks and cook, stirring occasionally, until they begin to soften, 3 to 4 minutes. Add the tomatoes and cook, breaking them up with a spoon, for 5 minutes.

> Add 6 cups water and bring to a boil. Stir in the sweet potatoes, kale, lentils, thyme, 1½ teaspoons salt, and ¼ teaspoon pepper. Simmer until the lentils are tender, 25 to 30 minutes.

> Spoon into bowls and top with the Parmesan, if using.

TIP

Basic brown lentils retain their shape better during cooking than pricier red and yellow lentils, so they're terrific for soups. Or you can substitute green lentils, which taste slightly peppery.

ginger chicken soup with vegetables

HANDS-ON TIME: 25 MINUTES | TOTAL TIME: 55 MINUTES | SERVES 6

2 tablespoons olive oil

1 small red onion, thinly sliced

3 cloves garlic, finely chopped

3 tablespoons grated fresh ginger

2 32-ounce containers low-sodium
   chicken broth

2 medium parsnips, peeled and chopped

2 medium carrots, peeled and chopped

2 stalks celery, thinly sliced

1 medium turnip, peeled and chopped
   Kosher salt

1 2- to 2½-pound rotisserie chicken

½ cup frozen peas

4 scallions, sliced

4 biscuits, store-bought or made from
   a mix (optional)

> Heat the oil in a large saucepan or Dutch oven over medium heat. Add the onion, garlic, and ginger and cook, stirring, until fragrant, 1 to 2 minutes.

> Add the broth. Stir in the parsnips, carrots, celery, turnip, and ½ teaspoon salt. Bring to a boil. Reduce heat and simmer until the vegetables are tender, 15 to 20 minutes.

> Meanwhile, using a fork or your fingers, shred the chicken meat, discarding the skin and bones.

> Add the chicken, peas, and scallions to the saucepan and cook until heated through, 3 to 4 minutes. Serve with the biscuits, if using.

classic split-pea soup

HANDS-ON TIME: 15 MINUTES | TOTAL TIME: 3 HOURS, 45 MINUTES | SERVES 6

1 ham hock
2 32-ounce containers low-sodium
   chicken broth
1 pound green split peas
2 large carrots, chopped
2 stalks celery, chopped
1 large onion, chopped
2 cloves garlic, chopped
1 bay leaf
1 teaspoon dried thyme
   Kosher salt

> Rinse the ham hock and place it in a large saucepan or Dutch oven along with the broth, split peas, carrots, celery, onion, garlic, bay leaf, thyme, and 1 teaspoon salt. Bring to a boil. Reduce heat and simmer, covered, stirring occasionally, until the vegetables are very tender, 3 to 3½ hours.

> Remove and discard the bay leaf. Transfer the ham hock to a plate and let sit until cool enough to handle, at least 10 minutes. Shred the meat and stir it into the soup.

TIP
Look for ham hocks in the meat case, near the bacon. If you can't find one, substitute ½ pound diced bacon. Fry it in the saucepan before adding the broth.

fisherman's soup

HANDS-ON TIME: 15 MINUTES | TOTAL TIME: 35 MINUTES | SERVES 4

1 tablespoon olive oil
2 leeks (white and light green parts), cut into ¼-inch-thick half-moons
2 cloves garlic, sliced
1 small fennel bulb, quartered and sliced
⅓ cup dry sherry
1 28-ounce can diced tomatoes
¼ teaspoon crushed red pepper
   Kosher salt
1 pound skinless halibut fillet or some other firm white fish, cut into 2-inch pieces
½ pound mussels, scrubbed
1 cup fresh flat-leaf parsley, roughly chopped
½ cup mixed olives

> Heat the oil in a large saucepan over medium-high heat. Add the leeks, garlic, and fennel and cook, stirring occasionally, until they begin to soften, 3 to 4 minutes.

> Add the sherry, tomatoes and their juices, red pepper, and 1 teaspoon salt and bring to a boil. Reduce heat and simmer for 15 minutes.

> Add the fish and mussels and simmer gently until the fish is cooked through and the mussels have opened, 4 to 5 minutes. Stir in the parsley. Serve with the olives.

TIP
Try this dish with lump crabmeat in place of the fish. Add the crab to the soup and simmer until heated through, 2 to 3 minutes.

butternut squash soup

HANDS-ON TIME: 25 MINUTES | TOTAL TIME: 50 MINUTES | SERVES 4

4 leeks (white and light green parts), chopped
1 3-pound butternut squash, peeled and
   cut into 1-inch pieces
1 bay leaf
5 cups low-sodium chicken broth
   Kosher salt and black pepper
2 teaspoons olive oil
1 tablespoon fresh rosemary, roughly
   chopped
¼ cup shelled raw pumpkin seeds, roughly
   chopped (optional)
1 baguette, sliced (optional)

> Place the leeks, squash, bay leaf, broth, ¾ teaspoon salt, and ¼ teaspoon pepper in a large saucepan or Dutch oven and bring to a boil. Reduce heat and simmer, stirring occasionally, until the squash is tender, 10 to 12 minutes.

> Remove and discard the bay leaf. Working in batches, puree the soup in a blender until smooth (or use a handheld immersion blender).

> Meanwhile, heat the oil in a small skillet over medium heat. Add the rosemary and pumpkin seeds, if using, and heat, stirring occasionally, until fragrant, 2 to 3 minutes.

> Divide the soup among bowls and top with the rosemary mixture. Serve with the bread, if using.

gazpacho

HANDS-ON TIME: 30 MINUTES | TOTAL TIME: 2$\frac{1}{2}$ HOURS (INCLUDES CHILLING) | SERVES 6

4 stalks celery, roughly chopped

3 red bell peppers, roughly chopped

3 small fennel bulbs, roughly chopped

2 beefsteak tomatoes (about 1 pound), diced
(or one 14.5-ounce can chopped tomatoes)

1 bunch scallions, roughly chopped

1 sweet onion, roughly chopped

2 cloves garlic, roughly chopped

4 cups tomato or vegetable juice

$\frac{1}{2}$ cup extra-virgin olive oil

$\frac{1}{3}$ cup fresh lemon juice

1 teaspoon hot pepper sauce (optional)
Kosher salt and black pepper

3 limes, halved

> Working in batches, place the celery, bell peppers, fennel, tomatoes, scallions, onion, and garlic in the bowl of a food processor and pulse until finely chopped but not pureed.

> Transfer to a large glass or plastic bowl and stir in the tomato juice, oil, lemon juice, hot sauce, if using, 2 teaspoons salt, and $\frac{1}{2}$ teaspoon pepper.

> Cover and refrigerate for at least 2 hours and up to 6. Serve chilled with the limes.

TIP
Upgrade this refreshing summer dish by adding chopped cooked shrimp or crumbled goat cheese as a garnish.

Ingredients for Greek Salad with Basil Dressing (recipe, page 44).

dinner salads

"Salad for dinner" doesn't have to be synonymous with "prelude to a craving for a huge slice of pie an hour later." In fact, salads—especially one of these big-bowl dinner versions— can be satisfyingly filling, as well as downright desirable. Combinations like shrimp with cherry tomatoes and chicken with sweet peaches will please health-conscious eaters and carefree carnivores alike. And about that piece of pie? Should the mood still strike, turn to page 186.

RECIPE KEY

🕐 30 MINUTES OR LESS

♥ HEART-HEALTHY

🍲 ONE POT

🌿 VEGETARIAN

✘ NO-COOK

🧸 KID-FRIENDLY

❄ FREEZABLE

tangy shrimp salad with summer vegetables

HANDS-ON TIME: 25 MINUTES | TOTAL TIME: 30 MINUTES | SERVES 4

1 pound large peeled and deveined shrimp
  Kosher salt and black pepper
1 pint grape or cherry tomatoes, halved
1 cucumber, cut into thin half-moons
1 red bell pepper, thinly sliced
1 cup fresh flat-leaf parsley sprigs
4 scallions, sliced
1 jalapeño, seeded and chopped
1 clove garlic, thinly sliced
3 tablespoons extra-virgin olive oil
1 tablespoon fresh lemon juice

> Bring a large saucepan of water to a boil. Add the shrimp and 1 tablespoon salt and cook until the shrimp are opaque throughout, 2 to 3 minutes. Drain and run under cold water to cool.

> In a large bowl, toss the shrimp, tomatoes, cucumber, bell pepper, parsley, scallions, jalapeño, garlic, oil, lemon juice, ¾ teaspoon salt, and ¼ teaspoon pepper. Let marinate for 5 minutes before serving.

TIP
To prepare this dish even faster, use precooked shrimp from the fish counter or the freezer case. Thaw frozen shrimp quickly by placing them in a colander and running under cool water.

chicken salad with herbs and radicchio

HANDS-ON TIME: 20 MINUTES | TOTAL TIME: 20 MINUTES | SERVES 4 TO 6

1 2- to 2½-pound rotisserie chicken
4 medium carrots, coarsely grated
6 scallions, thinly sliced on the diagonal
1 tablespoon fresh tarragon, roughly chopped
  Kosher salt and black pepper
½ cup extra-virgin olive oil
3 tablespoons white wine vinegar
2 teaspoons Dijon mustard
2 heads radicchio, leaves separated

> Using a fork or your fingers, shred the chicken meat, discarding the skin and bones. In a large bowl, combine the chicken, carrots, scallions, tarragon, ½ teaspoon salt, and ¼ teaspoon pepper.

> In a small bowl, whisk together the oil, vinegar, mustard, and ¼ teaspoon each salt and pepper.

> Divide the radicchio leaves among plates, top with the chicken mixture, and drizzle with the vinaigrette.

TIP
If you find radicchio too pep-
pery, spoon the salad into
Boston or Bibb lettuce leaves.
Or serve it in endive leaves as
a fork-free hors d'oeuvre.

creamy barley salad with apples

HANDS-ON TIME: 15 MINUTES | TOTAL TIME: 45 MINUTES | SERVES 4

½ cup pearl barley
   Kosher salt and black pepper
½ cup plain low-fat yogurt
 2 tablespoons extra-virgin olive oil
 1 tablespoon fresh lemon juice
 1 teaspoon Dijon mustard
 2 stalks celery, sliced
 1 apple, thinly sliced
¼ cup fresh mint, chopped
 2 bunches arugula, thick stems removed
   (about 6 cups)

> In a medium saucepan, combine the barley, 1½ cups water, and ½ teaspoon salt and bring to a boil. Reduce heat and simmer, covered, until the barley is tender and the water is absorbed, 25 to 30 minutes. Drain and spread on a rimmed baking sheet to cool.

> Meanwhile, in a large bowl, whisk together the yogurt, oil, lemon juice, mustard, ½ teaspoon salt, and ¼ teaspoon pepper. Add the celery, apple, mint, and cooled barley and toss to combine.

> Divide the arugula among bowls. Top with the barley mixture.

chicken and peach salad

HANDS-ON TIME: 20 MINUTES | TOTAL TIME: 20 MINUTES | SERVES 6

2 heads romaine lettuce, cut crosswise into 1-inch strips (about 12 cups)

1 2- to 2½-pound rotisserie chicken, meat thickly sliced

2 peaches, cut into 1-inch pieces

3 ounces blue cheese, sliced into pieces

½ cup almonds, roughly chopped

¼ cup white wine vinegar

¼ cup extra-virgin olive oil

Kosher salt and black pepper

> Arrange the lettuce, chicken, peaches, cheese, and almonds on a platter.

> In a small bowl, whisk together the vinegar, oil, 1 teaspoon salt, and ¼ teaspoon pepper. Drizzle over the salad.

TIP
This summery dish is great for a picnic or a concert in the park. Pack the vinaigrette separately and dress the salad just before serving.

Greek salad with basil dressing

HANDS-ON TIME: 15 MINUTES | TOTAL TIME: 15 MINUTES | SERVES 6

½ cup extra-virgin olive oil
1½ cups fresh basil
    Kosher salt and black pepper
2 14-ounce cans stuffed grape leaves
8 ounces Feta, broken into large pieces
1 seedless cucumber, peeled and cut
    into ¼-inch half-moons
1 cup cherry or grape tomatoes, halved
1 12-ounce jar pepperoncini, drained
1 lemon, cut into wedges
¾ cup olives, preferably kalamata

> In a blender, puree the olive oil, 1 cup of the basil, and ¼ teaspoon salt until smooth; set aside.

> Divide the stuffed grape leaves, Feta, cucumber, tomatoes, pepperoncini, lemon, olives, and the remaining ½ cup of basil among plates.

> Season the tomatoes and cucumbers with ¼ teaspoon each salt and pepper. Drizzle with the basil oil before serving.

TIP
Rice-stuffed grape
leaves are found in the
international-food section
of the supermarket.
Spicy pepperoncini will
be near the pickles.

spinach salad with warm onions and crispy salami

HANDS-ON TIME: 15 MINUTES | TOTAL TIME: 15 MINUTES | SERVES 4

2 tablespoons olive oil

¼ pound hard salami, cut into ½-inch pieces

2 tablespoons red wine vinegar

1 tablespoon Dijon mustard

1 tablespoon honey

Kosher salt and black pepper

½ red onion, sliced into rounds

2 bunches spinach, thick stems removed
(about 8 cups)

4 hard-boiled eggs (optional)

> Heat 1 tablespoon of the oil in a medium skillet over medium heat. Add the salami and cook, stirring occasionally, until browned, 2 to 3 minutes. Transfer to a paper towel–lined plate.

> Add the vinegar, mustard, honey, the remaining tablespoon of oil, and ¼ teaspoon each salt and pepper to the skillet with the drippings. Whisk to combine.

> Add the onion and cook, stirring occasionally, until it begins to soften, 3 to 4 minutes. Stir in the salami.

> Divide the spinach among plates and spoon the onion and salami over the top. Serve with the eggs, if using.

cool southwestern salad with corn and avocado

HANDS-ON TIME: 20 MINUTES | TOTAL TIME: 20 MINUTES | SERVES 4

2 small heads romaine lettuce, cut into
   bite-size pieces (about 12 cups)
1 cup corn kernels (cut from 1 to 2 ears,
   or frozen and thawed)
2 avocados, cut into 1-inch pieces
1 15.5-ounce can pinto beans, rinsed
½ red onion, thinly sliced
½ cup fresh cilantro
¼ cup extra-virgin olive oil
¼ cup fresh lime juice
½ teaspoon ground cumin
   Kosher salt and black pepper
½ 9-ounce bag tortilla chips

> In a large bowl, combine the lettuce, corn, avocados, beans, onion, and cilantro.

> In a small bowl, whisk together the oil, lime juice, cumin, ¾ teaspoon salt, and ¼ teaspoon pepper. Drizzle over the salad and gently toss. Serve with the tortilla chips.

TIP
Wrap the salad in a large
burrito or stuff it into a pita
for a portable meal.

Simple Roast Chicken (recipe, page 63).

poultry

Poor poultry—it has quite an image problem. Insult for a scaredy-cat? Chicken. Most embarrassing wedding dance? The Funky Chicken. A movie that bombs? A turkey. That ho-hum bird you've made a hundred times isn't helping, either. Help restore poultry's pluck with these boredom-free recipes, from Mediterranean-inspired chicken with juicy olives to turkey meat loaf with creamy mashed potatoes. Consider this a mealtime makeover. You get tasty, new dishes; poultry gets a whole new image.

RECIPE KEY

🕐 30 MINUTES OR LESS

♥ HEART-HEALTHY

🍲 ONE POT

🌳 VEGETARIAN

✖ NO-COOK

🧸 KID-FRIENDLY

❄ FREEZABLE

chicken with creamy spinach and shallots

HANDS-ON TIME: 20 MINUTES | TOTAL TIME: 35 MINUTES | SERVES 4

2 tablespoons olive oil

8 small chicken thighs (about 2 pounds)
   Kosher salt and black pepper

4 shallots, thinly sliced

¼ cup dry white wine

¼ cup sour cream

2 bunches spinach, thick stems removed
   (about 8 cups)

> Heat the oil in a large skillet over medium-high heat. Season the chicken with ½ teaspoon salt and ¼ teaspoon pepper and cook until browned and cooked through, 8 to 10 minutes per side. Transfer to plates.

> Spoon off and discard all but 1 tablespoon of the fat and return the skillet to medium heat. Add the shallots and cook, stirring, until they begin to soften, 2 to 3 minutes.

> Stir in the wine and sour cream. Add the spinach and ¼ teaspoon each salt and pepper. Cook, tossing gently, until the spinach begins to wilt, 1 to 2 minutes. Serve with the chicken.

TIP
This rich, sophisticated take on sautéed spinach is also great alongside seared steak, pork, or lamb.

golden chicken with tomatoes and olives

HANDS-ON TIME: 20 MINUTES | TOTAL TIME: 30 MINUTES | SERVES 4

1 cup long-grain rice

2 tablespoons olive oil

1 pound boneless, skinless chicken breasts,
  cut into 2½-inch pieces
  Kosher salt and black pepper

1 large onion, thinly sliced

1 pint grape or cherry tomatoes, halved

1 cup large pimiento-stuffed olives, quartered

2 cloves garlic, thinly sliced

¾ cup dry white wine

¾ cup fresh flat-leaf parsley, chopped

> Cook the rice according to the package directions.

> Meanwhile, heat the oil in a large skillet over medium heat. Season the chicken with ½ teaspoon each salt and pepper. Cook until golden brown, 3 to 4 minutes per side. Transfer to a plate.

> Add the onion to the skillet and cook, stirring occasionally, until soft, 5 to 6 minutes. Add the tomatoes, olives, and garlic and cook, stirring, for 2 minutes.

> Return the chicken to the skillet and add the wine. Simmer until the chicken is cooked through and the sauce has slightly thickened, 4 to 6 minutes. Stir in the parsley. Serve with the rice.

roasted chicken, apples, and leeks

HANDS-ON TIME: 10 MINUTES | TOTAL TIME: 55 MINUTES | SERVES 4

4 small, crisp apples (such as Empire or
  Braeburn), quartered

2 leeks (white and light green parts), halved
  crosswise and lengthwise

6 small sprigs fresh rosemary

2 tablespoons olive oil
  Kosher salt and black pepper

8 small chicken thighs and drumsticks
  (4 of each, about 2½ pounds total)

> Heat oven to 400° F. In a large roasting pan, toss
the apples, leeks, rosemary, oil, ½ teaspoon salt, and
¼ teaspoon pepper.

> Season the chicken with ½ teaspoon each salt and
pepper and nestle, skin-side up, among the vegetables.

> Roast until the chicken is cooked through and the
apples and leeks are tender, 40 to 45 minutes.

TIP
Roasting chicken with
fruit adds a rich,
caramelized sweetness
to the bird. Instead of
apples, try Bartlett
or Bosc pears.

bean and chicken sausage stew

HANDS-ON TIME: 15 MINUTES | TOTAL TIME: 15 MINUTES | SERVES 4

1 tablespoon olive oil

1 12-ounce package fully cooked chicken
   sausage links, sliced

2 cloves garlic, thinly sliced

1 19-ounce can cannellini beans, rinsed

1 14.5-ounce can low-sodium chicken broth

1 14.5-ounce can diced tomatoes

1 bunch kale leaves, torn into 2-inch pieces
   Kosher salt and black pepper

1 loaf country bread (optional)

> Heat the oil in a large saucepan or Dutch oven over
medium heat. Add the sausage and cook, stirring once,
until browned, 2 to 3 minutes. Stir in the garlic and
cook for 2 minutes more.

> Add the beans, broth, and tomatoes and their liquid
and bring to a boil. Add the kale and ¼ teaspoon each
salt and pepper and simmer, stirring occasionally, until
wilted, 2 to 3 minutes. Serve with the bread, if using.

TIP
Turn this stew into a
protein-packed chili by
adding a can each of kidney
beans and chickpeas.

chicken enchiladas with green salsa

HANDS-ON TIME: 35 MINUTES | TOTAL TIME: 40 MINUTES | SERVES 4

4 tablespoons canola oil

2 small zucchini, diced

1 small red onion, chopped

½ cup corn kernels (from 1 ear, or frozen and thawed)

1 2- to 2½-pound rotisserie chicken, meat shredded

1½ cups grated Monterey Jack (6 ounces)
   Kosher salt and black pepper

12 6-inch corn tortillas

1 pound tomatillos, papery husks removed

1 jalapeño, seeded

1 cup fresh cilantro

1 tablespoon fresh lime juice

½ cup sour cream (optional)

> Heat oven to 400° F. Heat 1 tablespoon of the oil in a medium skillet over medium-high heat. Add the zucchini, onion, and corn and cook, stirring, until the onion begins to soften, 3 to 5 minutes. Transfer to a large bowl.

> Add the chicken, Monterey Jack, 1 teaspoon salt, and ¼ teaspoon pepper. Mix to combine.

> Wipe out the skillet and heat the remaining 3 table-spoons of oil over medium heat. One at a time, cook the tortillas in the oil until softened, 10 to 15 seconds per side. Transfer to a paper towel–lined plate.

> Roll the chicken mixture up in the tortillas and place them in a large baking dish, seam-side down. Bake until heated through, 8 to 10 minutes.

> Meanwhile, in a food processor, pulse the tomatillos, jalapeño, cilantro, lime juice, and ½ teaspoon salt until finely chopped. Serve the enchiladas with the salsa and sour cream, if using.

TIP
In place of the tomatillo sauce, you can use a store-bought mild green salsa.

simple roast chicken

HANDS-ON TIME: 10 MINUTES | TOTAL TIME: 1 HOUR, 25 MINUTES | SERVES 6

1 onion, sliced
1 3½- to 4-pound chicken, giblets removed
2 tablespoons olive oil
   Kosher salt and black pepper
1½ pounds new potatoes, halved

> Heat oven to 450° F. Place the onion in a large roasting pan. Pat the chicken dry with paper towels. Tuck the wings under the chicken and place it on top of the onion. Rub the chicken with 1 tablespoon of the oil and sprinkle with ½ teaspoon each salt and pepper.

> Scatter the potatoes around the chicken, drizzle with the remaining tablespoon of oil, and sprinkle with ½ teaspoon each salt and pepper.

> Roast, tossing the potatoes once, until a thermometer inserted into a thigh registers 165° F, 50 to 60 minutes. Let the chicken rest at least 15 minutes before carving. Serve with the potatoes and onions.

TIP
Get a jump start on your
weeknight dinners by
roasting 2 birds at once.
Place them side by side in a
roasting pan and allow an
additional 15 to 20 minutes
of cooking time.

turkey meat loaf with mashed potatoes

HANDS-ON TIME: 25 MINUTES | TOTAL TIME: 1 HOUR | SERVES 6

♥

1½ pounds lean ground turkey
1 onion, chopped
1 bunch spinach, thick stems removed and
  leaves chopped (about 4 cups)
1 cup fresh flat-leaf parsley, chopped
½ cup whole-wheat bread crumbs
2 tablespoons Dijon mustard
1 large egg white
  Kosher salt and black pepper
¼ cup ketchup
2 pounds red potatoes, quartered
1 cup buttermilk
1 tablespoon extra-virgin olive oil
¼ cup jarred marinara sauce, warmed
  (optional)

> Heat oven to 400° F. In a bowl, combine the turkey, onion, spinach, parsley, bread crumbs, mustard, egg white, and ½ teaspoon each salt and pepper.

> Transfer the mixture to a baking sheet and form it into a 10-inch loaf. Spread with the ketchup. Bake until cooked through, 45 to 50 minutes.

> Meanwhile, place the potatoes in a large pot with enough water to cover and bring to a boil. Reduce heat and simmer until tender, 15 to 18 minutes. Drain the potatoes and return them to the pot. Mash with the buttermilk, oil, ½ teaspoon salt, and ¼ teaspoon pepper.

> Serve the meat loaf with the potatoes and the marinara sauce, if using.

chicken and bok choy stir-fry

HANDS-ON TIME: 15 MINUTES | TOTAL TIME: 25 MINUTES | SERVES 4

1 cup long-grain white rice

1 tablespoon canola oil

4 6-ounce boneless, skinless chicken breasts, cut into 1-inch pieces
    Kosher salt and black pepper

4 heads baby bok choy, quartered lengthwise

¼ cup low-sodium soy sauce

¼ cup store-bought barbecue sauce

4 scallions, thinly sliced

> Cook the rice according to the package directions.

> Meanwhile, heat the oil in a large skillet over medium-high heat. Season the chicken with ¼ teaspoon each salt and pepper and cook, tossing occasionally, until browned and cooked through, 4 to 6 minutes. Transfer to a plate.

> Add the bok choy and ¼ cup water to the skillet. Cover and cook until the bok choy is just tender, 3 to 4 minutes.

> In a small bowl, combine the soy sauce, barbecue sauce, and scallions. Add to the skillet and bring to a boil. Return the chicken to the skillet and cook, tossing, just until heated through, 1 to 2 minutes. Serve with the rice.

chicken souvlaki

HANDS-ON TIME: 25 MINUTES | TOTAL TIME: 30 MINUTES | SERVES 4

2 tomatoes, cut into wedges

¾ cup crumbled Feta (3 ounces)

½ small red onion, thinly sliced

¼ cup halved kalamata olives

5 tablespoons extra-virgin olive oil

2½ teaspoons red wine vinegar

1 tablespoon fresh lemon juice

1½ teaspoons dried oregano

Black pepper

1 pound boneless, skinless chicken breasts, cut into 2½-inch pieces

½ cup plain yogurt

1 small cucumber, diced

1½ tablespoons minced fresh dill

4 pieces flat bread or pitas, warmed

> In a medium bowl, combine the tomatoes, Feta, onion, and olives.

> In a large bowl, whisk together 4 tablespoons of the oil, 1½ teaspoons of the vinegar, the lemon juice, oregano, and ¼ teaspoon pepper.

> Pour 2½ tablespoons of the vinaigrette over the tomato mixture, toss, and set aside. Add the chicken to the remaining vinaigrette and toss to coat.

> Heat the remaining tablespoon of oil in a large skillet over medium-high heat. Transfer the chicken (but not the liquid) to the skillet and cook until golden brown and cooked through, 3 to 4 minutes per side.

> Meanwhile, in a small bowl, combine the yogurt, cucumber, dill, and the remaining teaspoon of vinegar. Serve with the bread, chicken, and tomato salad.

sweet and tangy wings with butter lettuce salad

HANDS-ON TIME: 15 MINUTES | TOTAL TIME: 35 MINUTES | SERVES 4

¼ cup apricot preserves
¼ cup balsamic vinegar
½ teaspoon ground ginger
¼ teaspoon cayenne pepper
   Kosher salt
3½ pounds chicken wings (about 25)
2 tablespoons extra-virgin olive oil
2 tablespoons store-bought pesto
1 tablespoon fresh lemon juice
1 head butter lettuce, torn into pieces

> Heat grill to medium-low. In a large bowl, combine the preserves, vinegar, ginger, cayenne, and ¾ teaspoon salt. Set aside ¼ cup of the mixture. Add the chicken wings to the large bowl and toss to coat.

> Grill the chicken, covered, turning occasionally, until cooked through, 25 to 30 minutes, basting with the reserved preserve mixture during the last 10 minutes of cooking.

> Meanwhile, in a small bowl, whisk together the oil, pesto, and lemon juice.

> Divide the lettuce among plates and drizzle with the pesto vinaigrette. Serve with the chicken wings.

TIP
If you don't have access
to a grill, you can cook the
wings in the broiler on
a sheet pan for the same
amount of time.

an at-a-glance guide to...chicken

How to read the label and choose the right cut for any dish.

The first step in making a delicious chicken dinner is buying the right kind of bird, but the claims made on the labels (what's natural? what's organic?) can be confusing. Urvashi Rangan, Ph.D., director of technical policy at the Consumers Union, in Yonkers, New York, explains the terms you see most often. For the next step—choosing the right cut—see the diagram opposite.

decoding the label lingo

NATURAL
No artificial ingredients were added during processing. But the bird might have been fed antibiotics.

ORGANIC
Raised without antibiotics, these chickens were given only organic feed (grown without synthetic fertilizers or pesticides), with no animal by-products.

CERTIFIED HUMANE
The chickens were raised in conditions that exceeded federal standards. They were fed no animal by-products and no antibiotics, except when ill.

FREE-RANGE
Although the term implies that the bird roamed free to eat a varied diet (which adds to the chicken's flavor, not to mention well-being), verification of this claim is not required. To be sure the chicken had access to the outdoors, look for both "free-range" and "certified humane" on the label.

KOSHER
These chickens were raised and slaughtered following Jewish dietary rules. Because kosher processing involves hand salting, the meat is often saltier than that of nonkosher birds.

WING
The boniest cut, the wing is considered white meat. It is made up of three sections, the first of which is sometimes sold separately as a "drumette."
Best for: Roasting, broiling, grilling, braising.

DRUMSTICK
This dark-meat piece is often sold with the thigh attached, labeled as a "leg." To separate the two parts, cut through the joint with a sharp knife.
Best for: Roasting, grilling, braising.

THIGH
Sometimes sold boneless, juicy dark-meat thighs are flavorful and hard to overcook.
Best for: Roasting, broiling, grilling, braising.

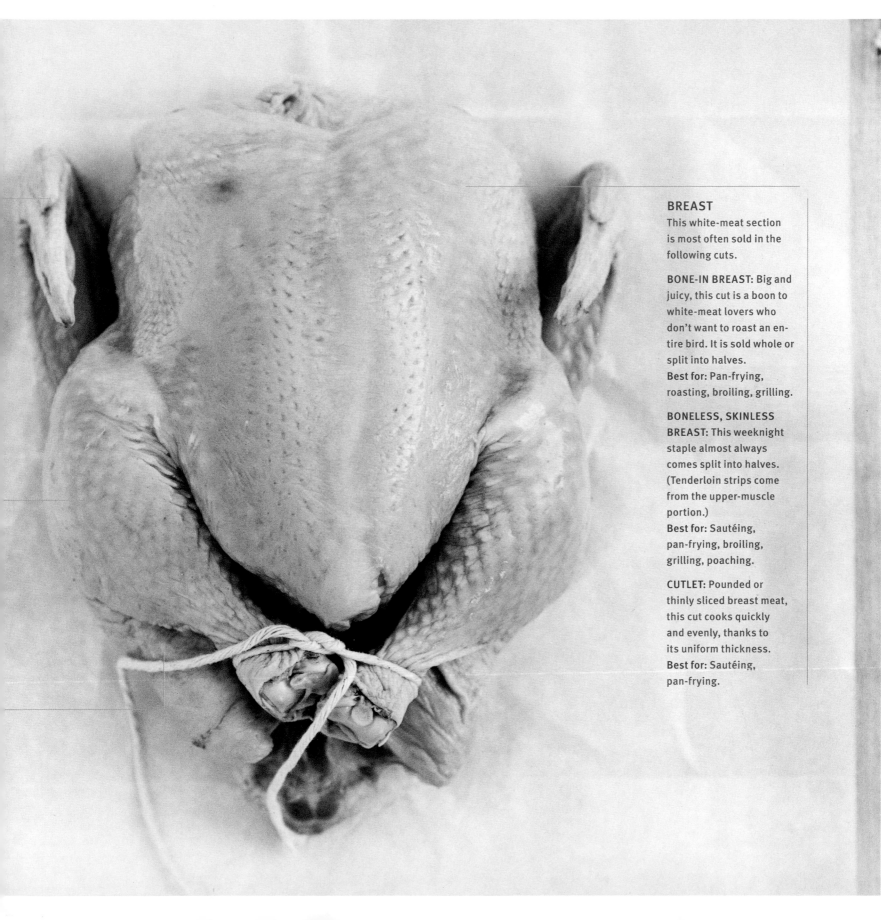

BREAST

This white-meat section is most often sold in the following cuts.

BONE-IN BREAST: Big and juicy, this cut is a boon to white-meat lovers who don't want to roast an entire bird. It is sold whole or split into halves.
Best for: Pan-frying, roasting, broiling, grilling.

BONELESS, SKINLESS BREAST: This weeknight staple almost always comes split into halves. (Tenderloin strips come from the upper-muscle portion.)
Best for: Sautéing, pan-frying, broiling, grilling, poaching.

CUTLET: Pounded or thinly sliced breast meat, this cut cooks quickly and evenly, thanks to its uniform thickness.
Best for: Sautéing, pan-frying.

Steak with Cauliflower and Crunchy
Bread Crumbs (recipe, page 80).

beef, pork, and lamb

It's always nice to have something juicy to talk about over dinner, and you can bet the main-dish meats in this chapter—great for special nights and every night—will make delicious conversation pieces. One reason: They're packed with flavor, like the sweet and savory dry rub on baby-back ribs or the fragrant oregano in mini beef burgers. Another: They're paired with talk-of-the town sides. On second thought, these easy but impressive dishes may leave your guests speechless.

RECIPE KEY

🕐 30 MINUTES OR LESS

♥ HEART-HEALTHY

🍲 ONE POT

🍄 VEGETARIAN

🔪 NO-COOK

🧸 KID-FRIENDLY

❄ FREEZABLE

skirt steak with lemon and chili-roasted potatoes

HANDS-ON TIME: 10 MINUTES | TOTAL TIME: 1 HOUR, 5 MINUTES | SERVES 4

1½ pounds new potatoes, halved
3 tablespoons olive oil
1 teaspoon chili powder
8 sprigs fresh thyme
   Kosher salt and black pepper
1½ pounds skirt steak
1 lemon, quartered

> Heat oven to 425° F. In a roasting pan, toss the potatoes, oil, chili powder, thyme, 1 teaspoon salt, and ¼ teaspoon pepper. Roast, stirring once, until golden brown and crisp, 40 to 45 minutes. Transfer to plates.

> Heat broiler. Wipe out the roasting pan. Season the steak with 1 teaspoon salt and ½ teaspoon pepper and place on the roasting pan. Broil the steak to the desired doneness, 3 to 4 minutes per side for medium-rare. Transfer to a cutting board and let rest for 5 minutes before slicing. Serve with the potatoes and lemon.

spiced mini burgers with couscous salad

HANDS-ON TIME: 25 MINUTES | TOTAL TIME: 25 MINUTES | SERVES 4

1   10-ounce box couscous (1½ cups)
1   pound ground beef
1½ teaspoons ground cumin
1½ tablespoons dried oregano
    Kosher salt and black pepper
4   tablespoons extra-virgin olive oil
6   scallions, sliced
4   plum tomatoes, quartered
1   seedless cucumber, cut into half-moons
3   tablespoons fresh lemon juice
1   8-ounce container hummus (optional)

> Place the couscous in a large bowl and pour 1½ cups hot tap water over the top. Cover and let stand for 5 minutes; fluff with a fork.

> Form the beef into 12 small ½-inch-thick patties. Sprinkle with the cumin, oregano, 1 teaspoon salt, and ¼ teaspoon pepper.

> Heat 1 tablespoon of the oil in a large skillet over medium heat. Add the patties and cook to the desired doneness, 4 minutes per side for medium.

> Toss the couscous with the scallions, tomatoes, cucumber, lemon juice, the remaining 3 tablespoons of oil, 1¼ teaspoons salt, and ¼ teaspoon pepper. Serve with the burgers and hummus, if using.

TIP
Turn this dinner into a Mediterranean feast by using ground lamb instead of ground beef for the patties and stirring ¼ cup crumbled Feta into the couscous salad.

steak with cauliflower and crunchy bread crumbs

HANDS-ON TIME: 15 MINUTES | TOTAL TIME: 25 MINUTES | SERVES 4

1 small baguette, torn into small pieces
   (about 2 cups)

3 tablespoons olive oil

2 tablespoons roughly chopped fresh
   flat-leaf parsley

1 tablespoon capers, roughly chopped

6 cloves garlic, unpeeled

1½ pounds strip steak
   Kosher salt and black pepper

1 head cauliflower, cut into florets

> Heat oven to 400° F. On a rimmed baking sheet, toss the bread with 1½ tablespoons of the oil. Arrange in an even layer and bake until golden and crisp, 5 to 6 minutes. Transfer to a bowl and toss with the parsley and capers; set aside. Reserve the baking sheet.

> Meanwhile, heat the remaining 1½ tablespoons of oil and the garlic in a large skillet (preferably cast-iron) over medium-high heat. Season the steak with ½ teaspoon each salt and pepper and cook until browned, 2 to 3 minutes per side. Transfer the steak to the baking sheet and roast to the desired doneness, 6 to 8 minutes for medium-rare. Let rest at least 5 minutes before slicing.

> Add the cauliflower and ½ cup water to the skillet and cook, covered, until the cauliflower is tender and the water has evaporated, 6 to 7 minutes. Sprinkle with the bread crumbs and serve with the steak and garlic.

TIP
Cooking the garlic in its skin flavors the cooking oil and leaves you with a tender clove inside. Squeeze it from the skin and eat with the steak or spread on toast for a quick, delicious hors d'oeuvre.

southwestern beef chili with corn

HANDS-ON TIME: 10 MINUTES | TOTAL TIME: 30 MINUTES | SERVES 4

1 tablespoon olive oil

2 carrots, chopped

1 onion, chopped

1 poblano or bell pepper, chopped

½ pound ground beef

2 tablespoons tomato paste

2 15-ounce cans black beans, rinsed

1 tablespoon chili powder

   Kosher salt and black pepper

½ cup corn kernels (from 1 ear, or
   frozen and thawed)

½ cup grated Cheddar (2 ounces)

2 scallions, sliced

> Heat the oil in a large saucepan over medium-high heat. Add the carrots, onion, and poblano and cook, stirring, for 3 minutes. Add the beef and cook, breaking it up with a spoon, until no longer pink, 3 to 5 minutes.

> Add the tomato paste and cook, stirring, until it is slightly darkened, 1 minute. Stir in the beans, chili powder, 3 cups water, ½ teaspoon salt, and ¼ teaspoon pepper. Simmer over medium heat until the vegetables are tender, 8 to 10 minutes. Stir in the corn.

> Divide the chili among bowls and top with the Cheddar and scallions.

TIP
Leftovers of this chili are an excellent addition to nachos. Spoon the chili on tortilla chips, top with grated Cheddar, and bake at 400° F until the cheese is melted.

pork with sautéed Granny Smith apples

HANDS-ON TIME: 20 MINUTES | TOTAL TIME: 30 MINUTES | SERVES 4

2 tablespoons all-purpose flour
1 teaspoon ground cumin
 Kosher salt and black pepper
12 pork cutlets (about 1½ pounds)
1 tablespoon canola oil
1 tablespoon butter
2 small Granny Smith apples, halved
½ cup low-sodium chicken broth
2 tablespoons white wine vinegar
¼ cup fresh flat-leaf parsley, chopped
2 tablespoons whole-grain mustard

> In a shallow bowl, combine the flour, cumin, 1 teaspoon salt, and ½ teaspoon pepper. Lightly coat each piece of pork with the flour mixture and set aside.

> Heat the oil and butter in a large skillet over medium-high heat. Sprinkle the apples with ¼ teaspoon each salt and pepper and cook, cut-side down, until golden brown, 3 to 5 minutes; transfer to plates.

> Working in batches (adding more oil if necessary), cook the pork until golden brown and cooked through, 2 to 3 minutes per side; transfer to the plates.

> Add the broth and vinegar to the skillet and simmer until slightly reduced, 4 to 5 minutes. Stir in the parsley. Serve the pork with the apples, pan sauce, and mustard.

TIP
In place of the cutlets, you can use four 6-ounce boneless pork chops, cooking them in one batch for 4 to 5 minutes per side.

dry-rubbed baby-back ribs

HANDS-ON TIME: 10 MINUTES | TOTAL TIME: 45 MINUTES | SERVES 4

4 cloves garlic, chopped
2 tablespoons brown sugar
1 teaspoon chili powder
½ teaspoon cayenne pepper
   Kosher salt and black pepper
2 racks baby-back ribs (about 3 pounds)

> In a small bowl, combine the garlic, brown sugar, chili powder, cayenne, 2 teaspoons salt, and ¾ teaspoon black pepper.

> Rub the spice mixture on the ribs and let sit for 10 minutes. Meanwhile, heat grill to medium.

> Grill the ribs, covered, turning occasionally, until cooked through, 25 to 30 minutes.

TIP
Try the spice mixture on flank steak, London broil, burgers, and pork tenderloin for a spicy-sweet kick.

roast pork and asparagus with mustard vinaigrette

HANDS-ON TIME: 30 MINUTES | TOTAL TIME: 30 MINUTES | SERVES 4

⅓ cup plus 2 tablespoons extra-virgin olive oil
1 pork tenderloin (about 1¼ pounds)
  Kosher salt and black pepper
1 pound asparagus, tough ends trimmed
3 shallots, cut into wedges
2 tablespoons cider vinegar
1 tablespoon whole-grain mustard

> Heat oven to 400° F. Heat 1 tablespoon of the oil in a large ovenproof skillet over medium-high heat. Season the pork with ¼ teaspoon each salt and pepper. Cook, turning, until browned, 5 to 6 minutes.

> Transfer the skillet to oven and roast until the pork is cooked through, 12 to 15 minutes. Let rest for at least 5 minutes before slicing.

> Meanwhile, on a rimmed baking sheet, toss the asparagus, shallots, 1 tablespoon oil, and ¼ teaspoon each salt and pepper. Arrange the vegetables in a single layer and roast, tossing once, until tender, 12 to 15 minutes.

> In a small bowl, whisk together the vinegar, mustard, and the remaining ⅓ cup of oil. Serve the pork with the vegetables and drizzle with the vinaigrette.

TIP
Take this recipe outside in the summer. Heat a grill to medium and cook the pork, covered, turning occasionally, for 20 minutes. Grill the asparagus and shallots (halved), turning occasionally, for 8 to 10 minutes.

sausage with warm tomatoes and hash browns

HANDS-ON TIME: 25 MINUTES | TOTAL TIME: 40 MINUTES | SERVES 6

4 tablespoons butter

1½ pounds russet potatoes, coarsely grated

1 onion, coarsely grated

½ cup fresh flat-leaf parsley, chopped
    Kosher salt and black pepper

2 tablespoons olive oil

12 small links sweet Italian sausage
    (about 2¼ pounds)

1 pint red or yellow cherry tomatoes, halved

> Melt the butter in a large skillet over medium heat. Add the potatoes and onion and cook, stirring occasionally, until they begin to soften, 4 to 5 minutes. Stir in half the parsley, 1 teaspoon salt, and ½ teaspoon pepper.

> Using a spatula, spread the potatoes, pressing them into the bottom of the skillet. Cook until a crust forms, 4 to 6 minutes. Break the potatoes apart, flip, and press down again. Cook until another crust forms, 4 to 6 minutes. Reduce heat to medium-low, cover, and cook until tender and crisp, 8 to 10 minutes.

> Meanwhile, heat the oil in a second large skillet over medium heat. Prick the sausages with a fork and cook, turning occasionally, until golden brown and cooked through, 15 to 20 minutes. Transfer to plates.

> Pour off all but 2 tablespoons of the fat from the second skillet. Add the tomatoes and ½ teaspoon each salt and pepper. Cook, tossing occasionally, until the tomatoes begin to soften, 2 to 3 minutes. Stir in the remaining parsley. Serve with the sausages and hash browns.

spiced lamb chops and smashed peas

HANDS-ON TIME: 20 MINUTES | TOTAL TIME: 20 MINUTES | SERVES 4

8 lamb chops (about 2 pounds)
1 teaspoon curry powder
  Kosher salt and black pepper
2 tablespoons olive oil
4 shallots, chopped
3 cups frozen peas, thawed
2 teaspoons fresh lemon juice
1 tablespoon chopped fresh mint
2 pieces pita bread, torn into quarters and
  toasted

> Heat oven to 400° F. Season the chops with the curry powder and ¾ teaspoon each salt and pepper.

> Heat 1 tablespoon of the oil in a large skillet over medium-high heat. Working in batches, brown the chops, about 2 minutes per side. Transfer to a baking sheet and roast to the desired doneness, 4 to 6 minutes for medium-rare.

> Wipe out the skillet and heat the remaining table-spoon of oil over medium heat. Add the shallots and cook, stirring occasionally, until soft, 2 to 3 minutes. Add the peas and gently smash with a fork or potato masher. Cook until heated through, about 2 minutes.

> Stir in the lemon juice, mint, and ¼ teaspoon each salt and pepper. Serve with the lamb and pita bread.

TIP
Any kind of lamb chop—rib (shown), loin, or shoulder—will work in this recipe. If you opt for shoulder chops, plan on only one per person, since they are larger than the others.

lamb chops with tomatoes and olives

HANDS-ON TIME: 20 MINUTES | TOTAL TIME: 25 MINUTES | SERVES 4

1 tablespoon olive oil
4 1½-inch-thick lamb loin chops
    (about 2 pounds)
1 teaspoon paprika
    Kosher salt and black pepper
4 shallots, halved
4 plum tomatoes, quartered
¼ cup pitted kalamata olives
¼ cup fresh flat-leaf parsley
1 baguette (optional)

> Heat oven to 400° F. Heat the oil in a large ovenproof skillet over medium-high heat. Season the lamb with the paprika, ¼ teaspoon salt, and ½ teaspoon pepper and cook until browned, 2 to 3 minutes per side.

> Add the shallots to the skillet, transfer to oven, and cook the lamb to the desired doneness, 6 to 8 minutes for medium-rare. Transfer the lamb to plates.

> Add the tomatoes, olives, and parsley to the hot skillet and toss with the shallots to combine. Serve with the lamb and bread, if using.

TIP
Paprika comes sweet, hot, or smoked. Any type will work in this recipe, but if you opt for hot, use only ½ teaspoon.

an at-a-glance guide to...beef, pork, and lamb

Whether the menu calls for a juicy steak or kid-friendly chops, here's all you need to know about the kindest cuts.

beef

FLANK STEAK
Flank steak is a lean, flavorful, and inexpensive cut. It is best served thinly sliced and is delicious in salads and sandwiches.
Best for: Pan-frying, broiling, and grilling.

GROUND BEEF
For tender, juicy burgers and meat loaf, choose ground chuck. Twenty percent fat is ideal (it's often labeled "80/20"); ground meat made from sirloin and other lean cuts tends to dry out and so is better suited for chili and meat sauces. When buying prepackaged ground meat, make sure it's bright red, not brown.
Best for: Pan-frying, roasting, broiling, and grilling.

SKIRT STEAK
Great for fajitas, this thin, flavorful cut has a loose texture that easily absorbs marinades and rubs. It typically comes as a long, narrow strip, so you may need to divide it into pieces to fit your pan.
Best for: Pan-frying, broiling, and grilling.

STRIP STEAK
Also known as New York strip, Kansas City strip, boneless club, and shell steak, this rich, tender selection is the quintessential steak-house cut. The tastiest pieces have a bright white marbling of fat that looks like a series of short, needle-thin lines. They melt away with cooking, rendering the meat lush and juicy.
Best for: Pan-frying, roasting, and grilling.

pork

BABY-BACK RIBS
Small and meaty, baby-back ribs cook quickly. This makes them a convenient alternative to larger, country-style ribs, which often require lengthy par-cooking in water. Two $1^1/_2$-pound racks will serve 4 people.
Best for: Roasting and grilling.

PORK CHOPS
Look for rich, meaty rib chops or loin chops, which look like little T-bone steaks. Boneless chops are tasty and lean but should be closely watched so they don't dry out during cooking. Whichever you choose, make sure they are at least an inch thick so they'll stay juicy.
Best for: Pan-frying, roasting, broiling, and grilling.

PORK LOIN
Boneless pork loin has a dense texture and a robust flavor. It can be stuffed and cooked as a roast or sliced into 1-inch-thick chops for pan-frying and grilling.
Best for: Roasting.

PORK TENDERLOIN
Pork tenderloin is a tender cut that's long and narrow, tapering at one end. Smaller than a pork loin, it cooks quickly and is an excellent choice for fast weeknight dinners. Figure on one $1^1/_4$-pound tenderloin for 4 people.
Best for: Pan-frying, roasting, and grilling.

PORK SAUSAGE
Ground pork sausage comes in a variety of sizes and already seasoned; flavors range from sweet to spicy. You can buy it out of the casing to use as an alternative to ground beef in meat sauce and stuffings or on pizza.
Best for: Pan-frying and grilling.

lamb

LAMB CHOPS
Lamb chops are sold in several cuts. As with the pork version, lamb loin chops look like little T-bone steaks, and they have a generous portion of meat. Pricier rib chops have a long bone on the side and are prized for their tenderness. Budget-friendly shoulder chops are larger and a bit chewier and fattier than the other varieties.
Best for: Pan-frying, roasting, broiling, and grilling.

LEG OF LAMB
Great for small crowds, a leg of lamb typically weighs between 8 and 10 pounds and serves 6 to 8 people. (Leftovers are delicious in sandwiches and salads.) Boneless legs are easier to carve than bone-in legs and are ideal for marinating and grilling; they're often stuffed with a mixture of garlic and herbs.
Best for: Roasting and grilling.

TOP ROUND LAMB
The top round, which comes from the leg, is frequently roasted whole and served thinly sliced. Because the meat is extremely tender, it can also be cut into steaks or cubed for kebabs.
Best for: Pan-frying, roasting, and grilling.

STRIP STEAK

PORK SAUSAGE

GROUND BEEF

Spaghetti with Quick Meat Sauce (recipe, page 115).

pasta

Pasta is like a best pal—the low-maintenance one you can rely on in a pinch, the one all your other friends actually like. With its infinite variety of shapes and sizes, it's the perfect base for everything from a hearty meat sauce to lemony vegetables. In this chapter, you'll find homey favorites, like macaroni and cheese, as well as no-fuss dressed-up dishes, like pasta with chicken, rosemary, and Parmesan. With any one of them, this pantry staple won't let you down. Isn't that what friends are for?

RECIPE KEY

🕐 30 MINUTES OR LESS

♥ HEART-HEALTHY

🍲 ONE POT

🍄 VEGETARIAN

✗ NO-COOK

🧸 KID-FRIENDLY

❄ FREEZABLE

linguine with tomato sauce

HANDS-ON TIME: 10 MINUTES | TOTAL TIME: 1 HOUR | SERVES 6

4 pounds tomatoes
¼ cup olive oil
2 cloves garlic, thinly sliced
  Kosher salt and black pepper
1 pound linguine
1 cup fresh basil

> Coarsely chop the tomatoes, reserving the juices. Heat the oil in a large saucepan over medium heat. Add the garlic and cook until fragrant, about 30 seconds.

> Add the tomatoes and their juices, 1½ teaspoons salt, and ¼ teaspoon pepper. Simmer, stirring occasionally, until the tomatoes break down and the sauce thickens, 45 to 50 minutes.

> When the sauce has 20 minutes left to cook, cook the pasta according to the package directions. Drain the pasta and return it to the pot. Add the sauce and basil and toss to combine.

TIP
To make the most of ripe tomatoes in summer, cook a double batch of this sauce and freeze half. Ladle the cooled sauce into resealable plastic bags, filling halfway. Freeze for up to 3 months.

Parmesan pasta with chicken and rosemary

HANDS-ON TIME: 15 MINUTES | TOTAL TIME: 15 MINUTES | SERVES 4

12 ounces orecchiette (about 3 cups)
 1 2- to 2½-pound rotisserie chicken
 2 tablespoons chopped fresh rosemary
¾ cup grated Parmesan (3 ounces)
   Kosher salt and black pepper

> Cook the pasta according to the package directions. Reserve 1¼ cups of the cooking water. Drain the pasta and return it to the pot.

> Meanwhile, using a fork or your fingers, shred the chicken, discarding the skin and bones.

> Toss the pasta with the chicken, rosemary, the reserved pasta water, ½ cup of the Parmesan, ½ teaspoon salt, and ¼ teaspoon pepper. Cook, stirring, over medium-low heat, until the sauce has thickened slightly, 2 to 3 minutes. Sprinkle with the remaining ¼ cup of Parmesan.

TIP
Using water from the pasta pot is a classic cook's trick. Starchy and salted, it makes a light, flavorful sauce when combined with cheese and herbs. It's also great for thinning pestos and marinaras.

lasagna-style baked ziti

HANDS-ON TIME: 10 MINUTES | TOTAL TIME: 40 MINUTES | SERVES 4

12 ounces ziti (about 4 cups)
1 tablespoon olive oil
1 large onion, chopped
2 cloves garlic, finely chopped
½ pound lean ground beef
  Kosher salt and black pepper
1 26-ounce jar marinara sauce
1 bunch spinach, thick stems removed
  (about 4 cups)
½ cup ricotta
½ cup grated Parmesan (2 ounces)
1 cup grated mozzarella (4 ounces)

> Heat oven to 400° F. Cook the pasta according to the package directions. Drain the pasta and return it to the pot.

> Meanwhile, heat the oil in a large skillet over medium heat. Add the onion and garlic and cook, stirring occasionally, until they begin to soften, 4 to 5 minutes. Add the beef, ¾ teaspoon salt, and ¼ teaspoon pepper and cook, breaking up the meat with a spoon until it's no longer pink, 5 to 6 minutes.

> Toss the pasta with the meat mixture, marinara sauce, spinach, ricotta, and ¼ cup of the Parmesan. Transfer to a 9-by-13-inch baking dish or 4 large ramekins. Sprinkle with the mozzarella and the remaining ¼ cup of Parmesan and bake until the cheese melts, 12 to 15 minutes.

TIP
If you prefer, substitute Italian sausage for the ground beef or chopped broccoli for the spinach.

ravioli with peas and shallots

HANDS-ON TIME: 15 MINUTES | TOTAL TIME: 20 MINUTES | SERVES 4

1½ pounds cheese ravioli (fresh or frozen)
2 tablespoons butter
2 shallots, thinly sliced
1 10-ounce bag frozen peas
1 teaspoon grated lemon zest
  Kosher salt and black pepper

> Cook the ravioli according to the package directions. Reserve ½ cup of the cooking water, then drain the ravioli.

> Meanwhile, heat the butter in a large skillet over medium heat. Add the shallots and cook, stirring occasionally, until soft, 2 to 3 minutes.

> Add the peas, lemon zest, reserved ravioli water, ½ teaspoon salt, and ¼ teaspoon pepper. Cook, partially covered, until the peas are heated through, 3 to 4 minutes.

> Divide the ravioli among bowls and top with the pea mixture.

spaghetti with bacon and eggs

HANDS-ON TIME: 15 MINUTES | TOTAL TIME: 25 MINUTES | SERVES 4

12 ounces spaghetti (¾ of a box)
8 slices bacon
4 large eggs
½ cup plus 2 tablespoons grated Parmesan
  (about 2 ounces)
  Kosher salt and black pepper

> Cook the pasta according to the package directions. Reserve ½ cup of the cooking water. Drain the pasta and return it to the pot.

> Meanwhile, cook the bacon in a nonstick or cast-iron skillet over medium heat until crisp, 6 to 8 minutes. Transfer to a paper towel–lined plate. Crumble when cool.

> Wipe out the skillet and return it to medium heat. Crack the eggs into the skillet and cook until the whites are set but the yolks are still runny, 3 to 4 minutes.

> Toss the pasta with the bacon, the reserved pasta water, ½ cup of the Parmesan, ½ teaspoon salt, and ¼ teaspoon pepper.

> Divide the pasta among bowls and top with the eggs. Sprinkle with the remaining 2 tablespoons of Parmesan.

TIP
For a picture-perfect
sunny-side up egg, break
the egg into a small dish
first, then slide it gently
into the pan.

pasta with broccoli rabe and sausage

HANDS-ON TIME: 15 MINUTES | TOTAL TIME: 25 MINUTES | SERVES 6

1 pound orecchiette
1 tablespoon olive oil
1 pound sweet Italian sausage, casings removed
2 cloves garlic, finely chopped
2½ cups low-sodium chicken broth
⅛ teaspoon crushed red pepper
1 bunch broccoli rabe
4 tablespoons butter, cut into pieces
1 cup grated Parmesan (4 ounces)
Kosher salt and black pepper

> Cook the pasta according to the package directions. Drain the pasta and return it to the pot.

> Meanwhile, heat the oil in a large saucepan over medium heat. Add the sausage and cook, breaking it up with a spoon, until it's no longer pink, 5 to 6 minutes. Stir in the garlic and cook 1 minute.

> Add the broth and red pepper and bring to a boil. Add the broccoli rabe and simmer, covered, until tender, 3 to 4 minutes. Stir in the butter and Parmesan and cook, uncovered, until the sauce thickens slightly, 1 to 2 minutes.

> Toss the pasta with the sausage mixture and ¼ teaspoon each salt and pepper.

TIP
Broccoli rabe is a leafy
distant cousin of broccoli
and has a tasty bitter flavor.
For a milder alternative,
substitute broccoli or
Swiss chard. For a more
peppery bite, try arugula
or radicchio.

macaroni and cheese

HANDS-ON TIME: 30 MINUTES | TOTAL TIME: 1 HOUR | SERVES 6

5 tablespoons butter, plus more
    for the baking dish
1 pound elbow macaroni
½ cup all-purpose flour
6 cups whole milk
2 cups grated Gruyère (8 ounces)
1½ cups grated Cheddar (6 ounces)
¼ teaspoon cayenne pepper
    Kosher salt

> Heat oven to 400° F. Butter a 9-by-13-inch baking dish or some other shallow 3-quart baking dish.

> Cook the pasta according to the package directions.

> Wipe out the pasta pot and melt the butter over medium heat. Add the flour and cook, stirring constantly, for 2 minutes (do not let it darken). Still stirring, slowly add the milk. Cook, stirring occasionally, until the sauce slightly thickens, 6 to 8 minutes.

> Add the Gruyère, Cheddar, cayenne, and 1½ teaspoons salt and cook just until the cheeses melt. Mix in the pasta. Transfer the pasta mixture to the prepared baking dish and bake until golden, 25 to 30 minutes.

spaghetti with quick meat sauce

HANDS-ON TIME: 30 MINUTES | TOTAL TIME: 30 MINUTES | SERVES 4

12 ounces spaghetti (¾ of a box)
2 tablespoons olive oil
1 large onion, chopped
2 carrots, chopped
2 cloves garlic, finely chopped
¾ pound ground beef
   Kosher salt and black pepper
1 28-ounce can crushed tomatoes
½ cup fresh flat-leaf parsley, chopped
¼ cup grated Parmesan (1 ounce)

> Cook the pasta according to the package directions.

> Meanwhile, heat the oil in a large saucepan over medium heat. Add the onion, carrots, and garlic and cook, stirring occasionally, until soft, 8 to 10 minutes.

> Increase heat to medium-high. Add the beef, ¾ teaspoon salt, and ½ teaspoon pepper and cook, breaking up the meat with a spoon, until it's no longer pink, 4 to 5 minutes. Add the tomatoes and simmer, stirring occasionally, until the sauce slightly thickens, about 5 minutes. Stir in the parsley.

> Serve the pasta with the sauce and sprinkle with the Parmesan.

TIP
Give this crowd-pleasing dish a healthy twist by replacing the beef with leaner ground turkey and the white-flour spaghetti with a whole-grain variety (to add fiber).

angel hair with spicy shrimp

HANDS-ON TIME: 15 MINUTES | TOTAL TIME: 15 MINUTES | SERVES 4

12 ounces angel hair pasta or spaghetti
   (¾ of a box)
 1 tablespoon olive oil
 2 cloves garlic, finely chopped
 1 pound peeled and deveined medium shrimp
¾ cup dry white wine
¼ teaspoon crushed red pepper
   Kosher salt
 2 tablespoons butter

> Cook the pasta according to the package directions. Drain the pasta and return it to the pot.

> Meanwhile, heat the oil in a large skillet over medium heat. Add the garlic and cook, stirring, for 1 minute (do not let it brown).

> Add the shrimp, wine, red pepper, and ½ teaspoon salt. Simmer until the shrimp are opaque throughout, 2 to 3 minutes. Stir in the butter. Toss the pasta with the shrimp mixture.

TIP
These spicy shrimp are also good served over rice or on top of broiled bread.

tortellini with eggplant and peppers

HANDS-ON TIME: 20 MINUTES | TOTAL TIME: 35 MINUTES | SERVES 4

2 tablespoons olive oil

1 medium eggplant, cut into ½-inch pieces

2 bell peppers, cut into ½-inch pieces

   Kosher salt and black pepper

4 cloves garlic, finely chopped

¼ teaspoon crushed red pepper

3 cups low-sodium vegetable broth

1 pound cheese tortellini (fresh or frozen)

½ cup fresh flat-leaf parsley, chopped

½ cup grated Parmesan (2 ounces)

> Heat the oil in a large skillet over medium-high heat. Add the eggplant, bell peppers, ½ teaspoon salt, and ¼ teaspoon pepper. Cook, stirring occasionally, until the vegetables begin to soften, 6 to 8 minutes.

> Add the garlic and crushed red pepper and cook, stirring, for 1 minute. Add the broth and tortellini. Simmer, covered, stirring occasionally, until the tortellini are cooked through and most of the broth is absorbed, 12 to 15 minutes.

> Stir in the parsley and ¼ cup of the Parmesan. Spoon into bowls and sprinkle with the remaining ¼ cup of Parmesan.

an at-a-glance guide to...pasta

Which shapes go best with which sauces? Here's how to use your noodles.

FARFALLE, BOW TIES
cooking time: 10 to 12 minutes
best for: tossing with sauce, salads
ideal sauces: cheese, olive oil, butter

SPAGHETTI
cooking time: 9 to 11 minutes
best for: tossing with sauce
ideal sauces: tomato, pesto, meat, seafood

RIGATONI
cooking time: 11 to 13 minutes
best for: tossing with sauce, baked dishes
ideal sauces: chunky meat or
vegetable, cream, cheese

ELBOW MACARONI
cooking time: 6 to 8 minutes
best for: baked dishes, salads, soups
ideal sauces: cheese, butter

ORZO
cooking time: 9 to 11 minutes
best for: salads, soups
ideal sauces: light tomato, olive oil, vinaigrette

FETTUCCINE
cooking time: 10 to 12 minutes
best for: tossing with sauce
ideal sauces: meat, cream, cheese

PAPPARDELLE
cooking time: 7 to 10 minutes
best for: tossing with sauce
ideal sauces: tomato, meat, vegetable

FUSILLI, ROTINI
cooking time: 8 to 10 minutes
best for: baked dishes, salads
ideal sauces: tomato, pesto, seafood

ANGEL HAIR
cooking time: 3 to 5 minutes
best for: tossing with sauce
ideal sauces: light tomato, olive oil,
cream, butter, seafood

SHELLS
cooking time: 10 to 12 minutes
best for: baked dishes, salads
ideal sauces: tomato, meat, vegetable,
cream, cheese, vinaigrette

PENNE
cooking time: 10 to 12 minutes
best for: tossing with sauce
ideal sauces: chunky tomato, meat,
vegetable, cream

ORECCHIETTE
cooking time: 10 to 12 minutes
best for: tossing with sauce
ideal sauces: meat, cream, seafood

ZITI
cooking time: 10 to 12 minutes
best for: baked dishes
ideal sauces: light tomato, olive oil,
cream, cheese

LINGUINE
cooking time: 10 to 12 minutes
best for: tossing with sauce
ideal sauces: tomato, pesto,
olive oil, seafood

JUMBO SHELLS
cooking time: 11 to 13 minutes
best for: stuffing, baked dishes
ideal sauces: tomato, cream

pasta protocol

Get separate, tender strands every
time by following these rules.

DO'S

■ Use a large, thin, lightweight pot that holds
at least 7 quarts. The lighter the pot, the faster
it will return to a boil after you add the pasta.

■ Salt the water once it comes to a boil.
(Add salt earlier and it can pit an aluminum
pot.) For every pound of pasta, figure on
2 tablespoons of salt and 6 quarts of water.

■ Stir the pasta right after you add it to the
water, then occasionally while cooking to
keep it from sticking together.

■ Test for doneness about 1 minute before
the time given on the package instructions.
Dried pasta should be cooked through but
still firm to the bite. Fresh pasta will rise
to the surface when it's ready; it should be
chewy and uniform in color throughout.

DON'TS

■ There's no need to break pasta to fit it
in the pot. Let the ends stick out until the
submerged sections soften, in about
1 minute. Then stir to bend the pasta and
push it underwater.

■ Don't add oil to the pot in an attempt to
keep the noodles from sticking together; stirring with a pasta fork is more effective. Oil
also prevents the sauce from coating the pasta
and makes cleanup a greasy proposition.

■ Don't discard all the cooking liquid. Before
draining the pasta, reserve ½ cup to add
to your sauce for seasoning or to adjust its
consistency.

■ Don't rinse cooked pasta. Besides eliminat-
ing the flavorful starch that helps the sauce
adhere, this cools the pasta.

Garlicky Broiled Salmon and
Tomatoes (recipe, page 132).

seafood

You may know your way around a salmon fillet, but when it comes to incorporating other fish into your diet, you sometimes feel as if you're swimming upstream. Fortunately, this chapter is packed with dependable, doable, delicious recipes. Yes, you'll find fresh ways to prepare salmon, but you'll also discover dishes like crispy breaded shrimp with rosemary and grilled mahimahi with grapefruit. Think of these as your new fast and foolproof weeknight staples—and go with the flow.

RECIPE KEY

🕐 30 MINUTES OR LESS

❤ HEART-HEALTHY

🍲 ONE POT

🌱 VEGETARIAN

✖ NO-COOK

🧸 KID-FRIENDLY

❄ FREEZABLE

crispy breaded shrimp with cannellini beans

HANDS-ON TIME: 20 MINUTES | TOTAL TIME: 20 MINUTES | SERVES 4

½ cup bread crumbs

2 tablespoons chopped fresh rosemary

5 tablespoons olive oil

Kosher salt and black pepper

1 pound peeled and deveined medium shrimp

1 clove garlic, chopped

1 19-ounce can cannellini beans, rinsed

2 bunches arugula, thick stems removed (about 8 cups)

> Heat oven to 400° F. In a large bowl, mix the bread crumbs, rosemary, 3 tablespoons of the oil, ½ teaspoon salt, and ¼ teaspoon pepper. Add the shrimp and toss to coat.

> Transfer the shrimp and any excess crumbs to a baking sheet. Bake until the shrimp are cooked through and the crumbs are crispy, 10 to 12 minutes.

> Meanwhile, heat the remaining 2 tablespoons of oil in a medium skillet over medium-high heat. Add the garlic and cook, stirring, for 30 seconds. Add the beans, ¼ cup water, and ¼ teaspoon each salt and pepper. Cook until heated through, 2 to 3 minutes. Remove from heat and toss with the arugula.

> Serve the bean mixture with the shrimp and sprinkle any remaining bread crumbs over the top.

TIP
Any sturdy herb works
well in this recipe.
In place of rosemary,
try sage or thyme.

baked cod and chorizo

HANDS-ON TIME: 25 MINUTES | TOTAL TIME: 45 MINUTES | SERVES 4

2 tablespoons olive oil

4 ounces Spanish chorizo (cured sausage), thinly sliced

1 pound Yukon gold potatoes, sliced ¼ inch thick

2 leeks (white and light green parts), cut into thin half-moons

¼ teaspoon crumbled saffron threads
Kosher salt and black pepper

1 1½-pound piece cod fillet

¼ cup fresh flat-leaf parsley, roughly chopped

> Heat oven to 400° F. Heat 1 tablespoon of the oil in a large ovenproof skillet over medium-high heat. Add the sausage and cook, tossing occasionally, until browned, 2 to 3 minutes.

> Add the potatoes and cook, stirring occasionally, for 10 minutes. Add the leeks, saffron, ½ cup water, ¾ teaspoon salt, and ⅛ teaspoon pepper. Bring to a boil.

> Season the cod with ½ teaspoon salt and ⅛ teaspoon pepper. Place it on top of the potatoes and drizzle with the remaining tablespoon of oil.

> Transfer the skillet to oven and bake until the cod is opaque throughout, 15 to 20 minutes. Sprinkle with the parsley before serving.

salmon and fennel with roasted-lemon vinaigrette

HANDS-ON TIME: 15 MINUTES | TOTAL TIME: 30 MINUTES | SERVES 4

2 bulbs fennel, thinly sliced

2 lemons, halved crosswise

4 cloves garlic, unpeeled

3 tablespoons olive oil

Kosher salt and black pepper

4 6-ounce pieces skinless salmon fillet

1 teaspoon honey

1 teaspoon chopped fresh rosemary

12 ounces mixed greens (about 8 cups)

> Heat oven to 400° F. In a large roasting pan, toss the fennel, lemons, garlic, 1 tablespoon of the oil, and ¼ teaspoon each salt and pepper. Roast until the fennel begins to soften, 6 to 8 minutes.

> Season the salmon with ½ teaspoon salt and ¼ teaspoon pepper and nestle in the fennel. Roast until the salmon is opaque throughout, 12 to 15 minutes.

> Squeeze the garlic out of the skins into a small bowl and mash to a paste. Squeeze the lemon pulp and juice into the bowl. Stir in the honey, rosemary, the remaining 2 tablespoons of oil, and ¼ teaspoon salt. Divide the greens among plates, top with the salmon and fennel, and drizzle with the dressing.

TIP

This dish is also delicious served at room temperature. Roast the salmon, fennel, and lemon and make the dressing in advance. Dress the greens and fish just before serving.

curried rice with shrimp

HANDS-ON TIME: 20 MINUTES | TOTAL TIME: 45 MINUTES | SERVES 4

1 tablespoon olive oil
1 large onion, chopped
2 carrots, chopped
2 cloves garlic, chopped
2 teaspoons curry powder
1 cup long-grain white rice
  Kosher salt and black pepper
1½ pounds peeled and deveined
  large shrimp
½ cup fresh basil

> Heat the oil in a large skillet over medium heat. Add the onion and carrots and cook, stirring occasionally, until soft, 6 to 8 minutes.

> Add the garlic and curry and cook, stirring, until fragrant, about 2 minutes.

> Add the rice, 2½ cups water, and ½ teaspoon each salt and pepper and bring to a boil. Reduce heat and simmer, covered, for 15 minutes.

> Season the shrimp with ½ teaspoon salt and ¼ teaspoon pepper and nestle them in the partially cooked rice. Cover and cook until the shrimp are opaque throughout, 4 to 5 minutes. Fold in the basil.

TIP
Upgrade this Indian-inspired dish with basmati rice, a fragrant long-grain variety with a delicate, fluffy texture.

garlicky broiled salmon and tomatoes

HANDS-ON TIME: 10 MINUTES | TOTAL TIME: 15 MINUTES | SERVES 4

4 6-ounce pieces skinless salmon fillet

4 medium tomatoes, halved

½ teaspoon paprika

2 tablespoons olive oil

 Kosher salt and black pepper

8 sprigs fresh thyme

4 cloves garlic, sliced

> Heat broiler. Place the salmon and tomatoes, cut-side up, in a broilerproof roasting pan or on a rimmed baking sheet.

> Sprinkle the salmon with the paprika. Drizzle the salmon and tomatoes with the oil and season with ¾ teaspoon salt and ¼ teaspoon pepper. Scatter the thyme and garlic over the top.

> Broil until the salmon is opaque throughout and the tomatoes are tender, 8 to 10 minutes.

TIP
This simple preparation lends itself to a variety of fish. Try it with halibut or striped bass.

halibut with lentils and mustard sauce

HANDS-ON TIME: 30 MINUTES | TOTAL TIME: 40 MINUTES | SERVES 4

2 tablespoons olive oil
1 large onion, chopped
2 cloves garlic, chopped
1 medium sweet potato, peeled and cut into
¼-inch pieces
2½ cups low-sodium chicken broth
1¼ cups green lentils, rinsed (½ pound)
Kosher salt and black pepper
4 6-ounce pieces skinless halibut fillet
¼ cup Dijon mustard
¼ cup dry white wine
1 tablespoon chopped fresh tarragon

> Heat 1 tablespoon of the oil in a large saucepan over medium heat. Add the onion and cook, stirring occasionally, until soft, 5 to 6 minutes.

> Add the garlic and sweet potato and cook, stirring, for 1 minute. Add the broth and lentils and simmer, covered, until the lentils are tender, 20 to 25 minutes. Season with ½ teaspoon each salt and pepper.

> Meanwhile, heat the remaining tablespoon of oil in a large skillet over medium-high heat. Season the fish with ¼ teaspoon each salt and pepper. Cook until opaque throughout, 3 to 5 minutes per side.

> In a bowl, whisk together the mustard, wine, and tarragon. Divide the lentils and fish among plates and drizzle with the sauce.

TIP
Tossed with the mustard
sauce, the lentils and
sweet potatoes make a
delicious side dish for
sausage, pork, or lamb.

poached scallops with leeks and carrots

HANDS-ON TIME: 20 MINUTES | TOTAL TIME: 30 MINUTES | SERVES 4

2 tablespoons olive oil

4 carrots, cut into thin strips

2 leeks (white and light green parts), cut into thin strips

½ cup dry white wine

12 large sea scallops (about 1½ pounds)

Kosher salt and black pepper

1 cup fresh flat-leaf parsley, finely chopped

1 clove garlic, finely chopped

2 tablespoons pine nuts, finely chopped

> Heat 1 tablespoon of the oil in a large skillet over medium-high heat. Add the carrots and leeks and cook, stirring, for 2 minutes. Add the wine and ½ cup water and bring to a boil.

> Season the scallops with ½ teaspoon salt and ¼ teaspoon pepper and place on top of the vegetables. Reduce heat and simmer, covered, until the scallops are opaque throughout, 6 to 8 minutes. Transfer the scallops to a plate.

> In a small bowl, combine the parsley, garlic, pine nuts, and the remaining tablespoon of oil. Stir into the vegetables and broth. Serve with the scallops.

TIP

Instead of chopping the parsley, garlic, and pine nuts by hand, pulse them in a food processor with 1 tablespoon of the oil.

grilled mahimahi with grapefruit, avocado, and watercress

HANDS-ON TIME: 20 MINUTES | TOTAL TIME: 20 MINUTES | SERVES 4

1½ pounds skinless mahimahi, cut into
    8 pieces
1 teaspoon plus 2 tablespoons extra-virgin
    olive oil
    Kosher salt and black pepper
1 grapefruit
2 tablespoons fresh lime juice
2 teaspoons honey
2 scallions, thinly sliced
2 bunches watercress, thick stems removed
    (about 6 cups)
1 avocado, cut into 1-inch pieces
1 baguette, sliced (optional)

> Heat a grill or grill pan to medium-high. Rub the mahimahi with 1 teaspoon of the oil and season with ¼ teaspoon salt and ⅛ teaspoon pepper. Grill until opaque throughout, 5 to 6 minutes per side.

> Meanwhile, with a knife, cut away the peel and white pith of the grapefruit. Cut the fruit into ¼-inch-thick rounds.

> In a small bowl, combine the lime juice, honey, scallions, ½ teaspoon salt, ⅛ teaspoon pepper, and the remaining 2 tablespoons of oil.

> Divide the mahimahi, watercress, avocado, and grapefruit among bowls and drizzle with the dressing. Serve with the bread, if using.

an at-a-glance guide to...seafood

From freshness to eco-friendliness, tips to help you get the best of the good stuff.

How to Buy Fish

LOOK AT IT
Fillets should be evenly colored, whatever color they are. If the edges show signs of fading or browning, or if the fillets are starting to gap or flake, the fish isn't fresh.

SMELL IT
As obvious as it may seem, trust your nose. The smell of fish should remind you of ocean breezes. If the piece you're considering smells distinctly fishy, it has been sitting around for too long.

FEEL IT
If the fish is wrapped in cellophane, you can use the thumb test. If the flesh doesn't spring back when you gently press on it, pass it by.

GET IT HOME SAFELY
Fish will spoil if left unrefrigerated for long, so make it the last thing you put in your cart. For a safe journey, ask the fishmonger to pack it with a bag of ice, or wrap it in a plastic bag and put it next to your frozen peas.

Shrimp 101

BUYING THEM
Shrimp are often sold by count per pound—the larger the shrimp, the fewer (and more expensive) they will be. Small shrimp come 41 to 50 pieces per pound; medium, 26 to 30; large, 16 to 20. In the supermarket seafood case, look for shrimp that feel firm, smell fresh, and are free of dark spots. But since they are almost always shipped frozen, then defrosted before they hit the case, you can save money and be better assured of freshness by buying bagged frozen shrimp. For best results, look for IQF (individually quick-frozen) on the label of any frozen fish or shellfish.

DEFROSTING THEM
To defrost shrimp, place them in a colander under cold running water or let them thaw overnight in the refrigerator.

PEELING THEM
Hold a shrimp in one hand. Slide the thumb of your other hand between the legs at the head end. Push your thumb under the shell and slide it around the body, separating the two. Leaving the tail on makes for an elegant presentation. To remove the tail, take two fingers and tightly pinch the section where the tail and the body are joined and pull the tail away.

DEVEINING THEM
With a sharp paring knife, make a cut about $\frac{1}{4}$ inch deep along the back of the shrimp down the length of the body. Remove and discard the vein and run the shrimp under cold water.

Picking the Right Fish for You and the Planet

COUNTRY OF ORIGIN
By law, this must be identified for fresh and frozen fish at the supermarket. A label marked U.S.A. is usually a good sign. "Our fisheries aren't perfect," says Tim Fitzgerald of the Environmental Defense Fund. "But we do have more safeguards in place than Asia or Latin America, where most of our other fish comes from."

MERCURY
Young children and women who are pregnant or plan to become pregnant should avoid fish that accumulate high levels of mercury and other toxins, like shark and imported swordfish. (See the Consumer Guide to Mercury in Fish at nrdc.org.)

FARMED VS. WILD
Some fish, like shellfish, striped bass, and catfish, thrive in responsibly managed farms. But other farmed fish, like imported shrimp and Atlantic salmon, are often crammed into pens, which breeds disease—which farmers then fight with large doses of antibiotics. Carnivorous farmed fish are fed great quantities of wild-caught fish, which contributes to overfishing. Wild fish aren't off the hook, however: Often they're caught in large nets or dredges, which deplete both their own population and those of other fish caught in the nets. There's no real nutritional difference between farmed and wild fish, and the toxin issue is too complex for simple answers.

THE BOTTOM LINE?
In general, opt for U.S. farm-raised seafood, but go wild with shrimp and salmon. For a complete guide to the human- and eco-friendliest fish, check out the Environmental Defense Fund's Seafood Selector at edf.org.

SHRIMP

SALMON

TUNA

Potato and Leek Flat Bread with
Greens (recipe, page 159).

vegetarian mains

Whether you're a strict vegetarian or a carnivore who occasionally likes to wander in leafier pastures, you'll find something here to keep you in the produce aisle longer. The meals in this chapter are healthy and will help you get your five-a-day, but they're hearty, too. So banish the thought that vegetables are only for side dishes. With recipes like deep-dish polenta pizza, the perfect quiche, and a creamy risotto made with sweet potatoes, you can veg out and still fill up.

RECIPE KEY

🕐 30 MINUTES OR LESS

♥ HEART-HEALTHY

🍲 ONE POT

🍄 VEGETARIAN

✖ NO-COOK

🧸 KID-FRIENDLY

❄ FREEZABLE

vegetarian mains

sweet potato risotto

HANDS-ON TIME: 45 MINUTES | TOTAL TIME: 45 MINUTES | SERVES 4

2 tablespoons olive oil

1 large onion, finely chopped
   Kosher salt and black pepper

2 small sweet potatoes (about 1 pound),
   cut into ¼-inch pieces

2 cloves garlic, chopped

1 cup Arborio rice

1 cup dry white wine

½ cup grated Parmesan (2 ounces)

2 teaspoons chopped fresh oregano

> Heat the oil in a large saucepan over medium heat. Add the onion, ½ teaspoon salt, and ¼ teaspoon pepper. Cook, stirring occasionally, until soft, 4 to 6 minutes. Add the sweet potatoes and garlic and cook, stirring occasionally, for 2 minutes.

> Add the rice and cook, stirring, for 2 minutes. Add the wine and cook, stirring frequently, until absorbed.

> Measure 3½ cups of water. Add ¾ cup at a time and cook, stirring occasionally and waiting until each addition is absorbed before adding the next. It should take 25 to 30 minutes for all the water to be absorbed.

> Stir in the Parmesan and oregano.

potato pierogi with sautéed cabbage and apples

HANDS-ON TIME: 20 MINUTES | TOTAL TIME: 20 MINUTES | SERVES 4

1 16.9-ounce box frozen potato-and-onion
   pierogi
1 tablespoon olive oil
1 small yellow onion, cut into rings
1 crisp apple (such as Braeburn or Gala),
   cut into ½-inch pieces
¼ small head green cabbage, shredded
1 tablespoon apple cider vinegar
   Kosher salt and black pepper
⅓ cup sour cream

> Cook the pierogi according to the package directions.

> Meanwhile, heat the oil in a medium skillet over medium-high heat. Add the onion and cook, stirring occasionally, until soft, 5 to 6 minutes. Add the apple and cook for 1 minute.

> Add the cabbage, vinegar, ½ teaspoon salt, and ¼ teaspoon pepper and cook, stirring, until the cabbage is slightly wilted but still crunchy, 2 to 3 minutes.

> Divide the cabbage mixture among plates. Serve with the pierogi and sour cream.

TIP
Pierogi are Eastern
European dumplings with
sweet or savory fillings.
Although they can be
boiled, pan-frying produces
a crispy exterior that
contrasts nicely with their
creamy interiors.

basic quiche

HANDS-ON TIME: 20 MINUTES | TOTAL TIME: 1 HOUR | SERVES 6

1 9-inch refrigerated piecrust

2 tablespoons olive oil

2 medium onions, chopped
  Kosher salt and black pepper

1 cup fresh flat-leaf parsley, chopped

4 large eggs

¾ cup half-and-half

⅛ teaspoon ground nutmeg

8 ounces Gruyère, grated

4 cups mixed greens

> Heat oven to 375° F. Fit the crust into a 9-inch pie plate. Place on a baking sheet.

> Heat 1 tablespoon of the oil in a large skillet over medium-low heat. Add the onions and ½ teaspoon each salt and pepper and cook, stirring occasionally, until soft, 5 to 7 minutes. Stir in the parsley.

> In a large bowl, whisk together the eggs, half-and-half, nutmeg, and ¼ teaspoon salt. Stir in the onion mixture and the Gruyère.

> Pour the egg mixture into the crust. Bake until a knife inserted in the center comes out clean, 35 to 40 minutes. Let sit for 5 minutes. Drizzle the greens with the remaining tablespoon of oil and sprinkle with ¼ teaspoon each salt and pepper. Serve with the quiche.

TIP
Tailor this quiche to your liking by stirring in a handful of chopped cooked ham, sautéed spinach, or steamed broccoli with the cheese.

deep-dish polenta pizza

HANDS-ON TIME: 15 MINUTES | TOTAL TIME: 45 MINUTES | SERVES 4

1 tablespoon olive oil, plus more for the pan

1 cup polenta (not instant)

¼ cup grated Parmesan (1 ounce)
    Kosher salt and black pepper

½ head radicchio, shredded

½ cup sun-dried tomatoes, thinly sliced

4 ounces mozzarella, cut into ½-inch pieces

> Heat oven to 400° F. Oil a 9-inch springform pan or pie plate; set aside.

> In a medium saucepan, bring 2¼ cups water to a boil. Whisking constantly, slowly add the polenta. Reduce heat to low and cook, stirring, until the polenta starts to pull away from the side of the pan, 4 to 5 minutes. Stir in the Parmesan, ½ teaspoon salt, and ¼ teaspoon pepper. Using a spoon, spread the polenta over the bottom and up the sides of the prepared pan.

> In a bowl, combine the radicchio, tomatoes, mozzarella, the remaining tablespoon of oil, and ¼ teaspoon each salt and pepper. Spoon the mixture over the polenta and bake until the polenta is crisp around the edges, 25 to 30 minutes.

TIP
This baked polenta crust can accommodate almost any pizza topping. Try arugula and prosciutto, cooked sausage and garlic, or caramelized onions and mushrooms.

creamy pesto gnocchi with green beans and ricotta

HANDS-ON TIME: 10 MINUTES | **TOTAL TIME:** 20 MINUTES | **SERVES** 4

1 pound gnocchi (fresh or frozen)
  Kosher salt and black pepper
½ pound green beans, cut into 1-inch pieces
  (about 2 cups)
1 8-ounce container store-bought pesto
  (about 1 cup)
¼ cup heavy cream
¼ cup ricotta

> Cook the gnocchi according to the package directions. Drain the gnocchi and return them to the pot.

> Meanwhile, bring a large saucepan of water to a boil and add 1 tablespoon salt. Add the green beans and cook until tender, 3 to 4 minutes; drain.

> Add the pesto and cream to the gnocchi and cook over medium heat, stirring, just until heated through, 2 to 3 minutes. Divide among bowls and top with the green beans, ricotta, and ¼ teaspoon pepper.

TIP
If you can't find gnocchi,
try this easy pesto-and-
cream sauce on tortellini.
And frozen peas are a fine
stand-in for green beans;
add them to the pasta
pot during the last 2 minutes of cooking.

vegetable fried rice

HANDS-ON TIME: 30 MINUTES | TOTAL TIME: 30 MINUTES | SERVES 4

1½ cups long-grain white rice

¾ cup low-sodium soy sauce

2 tablespoons light brown sugar

1 tablespoon rice vinegar

1 tablespoon grated fresh ginger

1 tablespoon canola oil

2 carrots, cut into matchstick-size strips

2 cups snow peas, cut into thirds

2 cups bean sprouts

4 scallions, thinly sliced

4 large eggs, beaten

> Cook the rice according to the package directions. Meanwhile, in a small bowl, combine the soy sauce, sugar, vinegar, and ginger.

> Heat the oil in a large nonstick skillet over medium-high heat. Add the carrots and cook, stirring, for 2 minutes. Add the snow peas, bean sprouts, and 3 tablespoons of the soy sauce mixture. Cook, stirring, until the vegetables are slightly tender, 2 to 3 minutes. Transfer to a bowl.

> Return the skillet to medium heat. Add the cooked rice, scallions, and the remaining soy sauce mixture. Cook until just heated through, 1 to 2 minutes.

> Push the rice toward the edges of the skillet. Pour the eggs into the center and cook, scrambling with a spatula, until set. Stir the eggs into the rice. Serve with the vegetables.

stewed-vegetable gratin

HANDS-ON TIME: 20 MINUTES | TOTAL TIME: 40 MINUTES | SERVES 6

3 tablespoons olive oil

1 medium onion, diced

2 stalks celery, diced

2 medium carrots, diced

1 14.5-ounce can diced tomatoes
   Kosher salt and black pepper

1 bunch Swiss chard, stems removed and
   leaves cut crosswise into 1-inch strips

1 19-ounce can cannellini beans, rinsed

1 cup plus 2 tablespoons grated Parmesan
   (about 4 ounces)

1 baguette, ends trimmed

2 tablespoons fresh thyme

> Heat oven to 400° F. Heat 1 tablespoon of the oil in a large saucepan over medium-high heat. Add the onion, celery, and carrots and cook, stirring occasionally, until the vegetables begin to soften, 3 to 4 minutes.

> Add the tomatoes and their liquid, ½ cup water, 1 teaspoon salt, and ¼ teaspoon pepper and bring to a boil. Add the Swiss chard and simmer, stirring, just until wilted, 1 to 2 minutes. Stir in the beans and 1 cup of the Parmesan. Transfer to an 8-by-11-inch baking dish or a shallow 2-quart casserole.

> Cut the baguette in half crosswise, then lengthwise, into ¼-inch-thick slices. Brush one side of each slice with the remaining 2 tablespoons of oil. Arrange the slices, oiled-side up, over the casserole, overlapping them slightly. Sprinkle with the thyme and the remaining 2 tablespoons of Parmesan. Bake until the bread is golden brown, 15 to 20 minutes.

potato and leek flat bread with greens

HANDS-ON TIME: 10 MINUTES │ **TOTAL TIME:** 35 MINUTES │ **SERVES 4**

Flour for the work surface
1 pound refrigerated pizza dough
   Cornmeal for the pan
2 small leeks (white and light green parts),
   cut into thin strips
2 medium red potatoes (about ¾ pound),
   thinly sliced
1 teaspoon fresh thyme
3 tablespoons extra-virgin olive oil
   Kosher salt and black pepper
¼ cup grated Gruyère (1 ounce)
4 cups mixed greens

> Heat oven to 450° F. On a lightly floured surface, roll and stretch the dough into a ¼-inch-thick circle or rectangle. Sprinkle a baking sheet with cornmeal and place the dough on top.

> In a large bowl, combine the leeks, potatoes, thyme, 1½ tablespoons of the oil, ¾ teaspoon salt, and ½ teaspoon pepper. Scatter the vegetable mixture over the dough and sprinkle with the Gruyère. Bake until the crust is golden and the potatoes are tender, 20 to 25 minutes. Cut into pieces.

> Drizzle the greens with the remaining 1½ table-spoons of oil and season with ¼ teaspoon each salt and pepper. Serve with the flat bread.

TIP
To clean leeks, which tend
to be gritty, cut them,
then swirl them in a bowl
of cold water. The sand will
sink to the bottom. Scoop
the leeks out and transfer
to a colander to drain.

an at-a-glance guide to...produce

Here's how to select and keep the tastiest vegetables in the market.

ARUGULA

How to choose: Fresh arugula has long, bright green leaves. Buy it with the roots intact if you can.

How to store: Wrap arugula sold in bunches in a moistened paper towel and place in a plastic bag before refrigerating. Loose leaves can go in a bag without a towel. Both types will last for up to 3 days. Refer to the label for packaged arugula's expiration date.

ASPARAGUS

How to choose: The stems should be firm and straight, the buds (or tips) tightly closed. Look for bright green or purple coloring, and avoid spears that are rubbery or wet or that have thick, woody stalks.

How to store: Wrap the ends in a damp paper towel and refrigerate in a plastic bag for up to 3 days.

BROCCOLI

How to choose: Pick broccoli with tight, compact florets that are an even dark green and firm stalks that are slightly lighter in color. A whitish stalk will be tough and woody.

How to store: Refrigerate in a plastic bag for up to 5 days.

BRUSSELS SPROUTS

How to choose: Look for firm, compact heads with clean stem ends. The sprouts should be no larger than 1 inch in diameter; any bigger and they'll taste too cabbagey.

How to store: Refrigerate sprouts in a tightly sealed plastic bag for up to 4 days.

BUTTERNUT SQUASH

How to choose: Pick a squash that is rock-solid and heavy for its size. The skin should be dull, not shiny (which is a sign the squash wasn't ripe when it was picked).

How to store: Keep in a cool, dry place (not in the refrigerator) for up to a month.

CABBAGE

How to choose: A head should feel firm and heavy for its size. The leaves should be tightly packed and shiny; their color should go from green to almost white or (for red cabbage) be a deep purple.

How to store: Refrigerate a head in a plastic bag for up to 1 week. Sprinkle water on cut pieces and refrigerate in a bag for up to 2 days.

CORN

How to choose: If you're not allowed to shuck, squeeze the ear to make sure the kernels are closely spaced, firm, and round. Look for a grassy green, tightly wrapped husk. The silk should be glossy and pale yellow, the stem moist.

How to store: Refrigerate ears unshucked in a plastic bag for up to 3 days.

EGGPLANT

How to choose: An eggplant should feel heavy for its size and is tastiest at less than 1$\frac{1}{2}$ pounds. (Larger, older ones tend to be bitter.) Look for a smooth, shiny dark purple skin and a green stem with leaves clinging to the top.

How to store: Refrigerate in a plastic bag for up to 5 days.

GREEN BEANS

How to choose: Look for bright green beans that are smooth and crisp with a velvety skin. Bend one in half to make sure it snaps. If you can see the beans clearly through the pods, they were picked past their prime.

How to store: Refrigerate in a plastic bag for up to 5 days.

MUSHROOMS

How to choose: Select firm, evenly colored mushrooms. They should have a smooth, dry skin and tightly closed caps.

How to store: Remove from any packaging. Refrigerate in a paper bag or wrapped in a damp paper towel for up to 3 days, and up to 1 week for shiitake and cremini varieties.

PARSNIPS

How to choose: Look for small to medium-size creamy white parsnips that are smooth, firm, and free of pitting. Limpness and shriveled ends are signs that parsnips will taste tough and woody.

How to store: Refrigerate in a plastic bag for up to 2 weeks.

PEPPERS

How to choose: Red bell peppers are simply mature green peppers; yellow and orange bell peppers are different, sweeter varieties. Keep an eye out for firm peppers with shiny, wrinkle-free skins.

How to store: Refrigerate peppers in a plastic bag. Red and yellow peppers will last for up to 5 days; green, about a week.

POTATOES

How to choose: Choose firm, smooth potatoes with few eyes. Avoid those with green patches—a sign of long exposure to light. These spots taste bitter and are toxic if eaten in large quantities.

How to store: Keep in an open paper bag in a cool, dry, ventilated place (not in the refrigerator) for up to 2 weeks. New potatoes will last for up to 5 days.

SPINACH

How to choose: Crinkly spinach is more flavorful (but slightly tougher) than the flat-leaf variety. For either, look for a dark color and unbroken leaves.

How to store: Refrigerate loosely wrapped in a plastic bag for up to 3 days. For packaged spinach, refer to the label.

SUMMER SQUASH

How to choose: Select yellow squash and zucchini that are less than 8 inches long. (Larger, older ones tend to be bitter.) Make sure the squash have bright skins and are firm, particularly at the stems.

How to store: Refrigerate in a plastic bag for up to 5 days.

TOMATOES

How to choose: Select tomatoes that are deeply colored and firm, with a little give, and that have a sweet, woody smell. Check grape tomatoes for wrinkles, a sign of age.

How to store: Keep tomatoes at room temperature on a plate for up to 3 days.

Roasted Parsnips and Carrots with Sage (recipe, page 175).

side dishes

When the dinner plates still bloom with green florets at the end of a meal, you know that the steamed broccoli that was keeping your go-to chicken dish company has worn out its welcome. Good news: The recipes in this chapter offer a fresh take on accessorizing your main dish. With flavorful sides like roast potatoes with Parmesan, couscous with an apricot vinaigrette, and Brussels sprouts with bacon, the only thing blooming at the table will be smiles.

RECIPE KEY

🕐 30 MINUTES OR LESS

♥ HEART-HEALTHY

🍲 ONE POT

🌱 VEGETARIAN

✖ NO-COOK

🧸 KID-FRIENDLY

❄ FREEZABLE

sautéed tomatoes and shallots

HANDS-ON TIME: 10 MINUTES |
TOTAL TIME: 20 MINUTES | SERVES 8

1 tablespoon olive oil
6 shallots, quartered
3 pints grape tomatoes
   Kosher salt and black pepper
½ cup dry white wine
2 tablespoons capers

> Heat the oil in a large skillet over medium-high heat. Add the shallots and cook, stirring occasionally, until they begin to soften, 4 to 5 minutes.

> Add the tomatoes, ¾ teaspoon salt, and ½ teaspoon pepper and cook, stirring, until a few of the tomatoes begin to burst, 2 to 3 minutes.

> Add the wine and cook until nearly evaporated, 4 to 5 minutes. Stir in the capers.

couscous with apricot vinaigrette

HANDS-ON TIME: 15 MINUTES |
TOTAL TIME: 15 MINUTES | SERVES 6

1 10-ounce box couscous (1½ cups)
¼ cup apricot preserves
3 tablespoons olive oil
2 tablespoons white wine vinegar
  Kosher salt and black pepper
2 scallions, chopped
¼ cup roasted almonds, chopped

> Place the couscous in a serving bowl. Pour 1½ cups hot tap water over the top. Cover and let stand for 5 minutes.

> Meanwhile, warm the preserves in a small saucepan over medium heat. Remove from heat and whisk in the oil, vinegar, 1 teaspoon salt, and ¼ teaspoon pepper.

> Fluff the couscous with a fork and toss with the scallions, almonds, and vinaigrette.

broiled asparagus

HANDS-ON TIME: 10 MINUTES |
TOTAL TIME: 10 MINUTES | SERVES 4

1 pound asparagus, trimmed
2 tablespoons olive oil
   Kosher salt and black pepper

> Heat broiler. On a baking sheet, toss the
asparagus with the oil and ¼ teaspoon each salt
and pepper.

> Arrange the asparagus in a single layer and
broil, shaking the baking sheet occasionally, until
tender and slightly charred, 6 to 8 minutes.

TIP
Upgrade this side dish
by topping it with
crumbled goat cheese
or shaved Parmesan
or pecorino.

Parmesan roasted potatoes

HANDS-ON TIME: 10 MINUTES |
TOTAL TIME: 1 HOUR | SERVES 4

2 pounds medium red potatoes, cut into 1-inch pieces
8 sprigs fresh thyme
1 cup grated Parmesan (4 ounces)
¼ cup olive oil
   Kosher salt and black pepper

> Heat oven to 400° F. In a large roasting pan, toss the potatoes, thyme, Parmesan, oil, 1 teaspoon salt, and ¼ teaspoon pepper.

> Roast, stirring once, until golden brown and crisp, 45 to 50 minutes.

TIP
These potatoes are delicious at room temperature, making them perfect for a buffet or a picnic or as an unexpected hors d'oeuvre, served with pesto for dipping.

coleslaw with caraway and raisins

HANDS-ON TIME: 10 MINUTES |
TOTAL TIME: 10 MINUTES | SERVES 4

¾ cup sour cream
2 tablespoons red wine vinegar
1 teaspoon caraway seeds
   Kosher salt and black pepper
1 small head green cabbage, cored and thinly sliced
   (about 6 cups)
6 scallions, thinly sliced
2 carrots, coarsely grated
1 cup golden raisins

> In a large bowl, whisk together the sour cream, vinegar, caraway seeds, ½ teaspoon salt, and ¼ teaspoon pepper.

> Add the cabbage, scallions, carrots, and raisins and toss to coat.

parsleyed corn on the cob

HANDS-ON TIME: 5 MINUTES |
TOTAL TIME: 15 MINUTES | SERVES 6

6 ears corn, shucked and halved
4 tablespoons butter, melted
¼ cup fresh flat-leaf parsley, roughly chopped
    Kosher salt and black pepper

> Bring a large pot of water to a boil. Add the corn and simmer just until tender, 3 to 5 minutes. Drain and transfer to a serving dish.

> Pour the butter over the corn and sprinkle with the parsley, ½ teaspoon salt, and ¼ teaspoon pepper.

TIP
If you're making burgers
and hot dogs on the
grill, throw the shucked
corn on, too. Cook, turn-
ing occasionally, until
charred, 6 to 8 minutes.

new potato and watercress salad

HANDS-ON TIME: 15 MINUTES │
TOTAL TIME: 35 MINUTES │ SERVES 8

4 pounds new potatoes
Kosher salt and black pepper
5 large eggs
1 cup mayonnaise
1 cup plain yogurt
2 tablespoons fresh lemon juice
1 tablespoon Dijon mustard
2 shallots, finely chopped
1 clove garlic, finely chopped
1 cup watercress, torn into 2-inch pieces
¼ cup chopped fresh chives

> Place the potatoes in a large pot with enough cold water to cover and bring to a boil. Add 1 tablespoon salt, reduce heat, and simmer until tender, 15 to 18 minutes. Drain, run under cold water to cool, and cut in half.

> Meanwhile, place the eggs in a large saucepan with enough cold water to cover. Bring to a boil. Remove from heat, cover the saucepan, and let stand for 12 minutes. Drain and run under cold water to cool. Peel and roughly chop.

> In a large bowl, whisk together the mayonnaise, yogurt, lemon juice, mustard, shallots, garlic, ½ teaspoon salt, and ¼ teaspoon pepper until smooth.

> Add the potatoes, eggs, watercress, and chives and toss to coat.

sautéed zucchini

HANDS-ON TIME: 25 MINUTES |
TOTAL TIME: 35 MINUTES | SERVES 6

2 tablespoons olive oil
4 medium zucchini, thinly sliced
2 cloves garlic, finely chopped
1 tablespoon fresh oregano or marjoram, chopped
   Kosher salt and black pepper

> Heat 1 tablespoon of the oil in a large skillet
over medium-high heat. Add half the zucchini and
cook, stirring twice, until golden brown, 10 to 12
minutes. Transfer to a plate and repeat with the
remaining tablespoon of oil and zucchini.

> Return the first batch of zucchini to the skillet
along with the garlic, oregano, ½ teaspoon salt,
and ¼ teaspoon pepper. Cook, tossing gently, until
the garlic is fragrant, 1 to 2 minutes.

TIP
Use leftovers of this
garlicky dish as a topper
for pasta or fold them
into scrambled eggs.

wheat berry salad with bacon

HANDS-ON TIME: 20 MINUTES |
TOTAL TIME: 1 HOUR, 15 MINUTES | SERVES 6

1	cup wheat berries
	Kosher salt and black pepper
½	cup pecan halves
6	slices bacon
½	cup dried cherries
½	cup fresh flat-leaf parsley
2	shallots, thinly sliced
2	tablespoons extra-virgin olive oil
2	tablespoons fresh lemon juice

> In a large saucepan, combine the wheat berries, 4 quarts water, and 1 teaspoon salt and bring to a boil. Cook until tender but still slightly chewy, 50 to 60 minutes. Drain and rinse with cold water to cool. Transfer to a large bowl.

> Meanwhile, heat oven to 350° F. Spread the pecans on a rimmed baking sheet and bake, tossing occasionally, until fragrant and toasted, 6 to 8 minutes. Let cool, then roughly chop.

> Meanwhile, cook the bacon in a large skillet over medium-high heat until crisp, 6 to 8 minutes. Transfer to a paper towel–lined plate. When cool, crumble and add to the wheat berries, along with the pecans, cherries, parsley, shallots, oil, lemon juice, and ¼ teaspoon each salt and pepper. Stir gently to combine.

Cheddar and scallion grits

HANDS-ON TIME: 10 MINUTES |
TOTAL TIME: 30 MINUTES | SERVES 4

Kosher salt and black pepper
1 cup grits (not instant or quick cooking)
1 cup grated white Cheddar (4 ounces)
2 scallions, thinly sliced
1 tablespoon butter

> In a medium saucepan, bring 4¼ cups water to a boil. Add 1½ teaspoons salt. Slowly whisk in the grits. Reduce heat to low and cook, whisking frequently, until the grits thicken and pull away from the side of the pan, 15 to 20 minutes.

> Add the Cheddar and stir until melted. Top with the scallions, butter, and ¼ teaspoon pepper.

TIP
Turn this into a main course by adding sautéed shrimp or andouille sausage.

Brussels sprouts with bacon and golden raisins

HANDS-ON TIME: 15 MINUTES |
TOTAL TIME: 45 MINUTES | SERVES 8

½ cup cider vinegar
½ cup golden raisins
2 pounds small Brussels sprouts, trimmed and halved
2 tablespoons olive oil
  Kosher salt and black pepper
6 slices bacon
1 small red onion, cut into thin half-moons

> Heat oven to 425° F. Warm the vinegar in a small saucepan over medium heat. Remove from heat, add the raisins, and let sit for 15 minutes; drain.

> On a large rimmed baking sheet, toss the Brussels sprouts, oil, and 1 teaspoon each salt and pepper. Roast, stirring once, until tender and slightly golden, 25 to 30 minutes.

> Meanwhile, cook the bacon in a large skillet over medium-high heat until crisp, 6 to 8 minutes. Transfer to a paper towel–lined plate; crumble. Discard all but 2 tablespoons of the drippings.

> Return the skillet to medium heat. Add the onion and cook, stirring occasionally, until tender, 5 to 6 minutes. Add the Brussels sprouts, raisins, and bacon and toss to combine.

roasted parsnips and carrots with sage

HANDS-ON TIME: 15 MINUTES |
TOTAL TIME: 1 HOUR, 10 MINUTES | SERVES 8

1½ pounds parsnips, peeled and cut into thin strips
1½ pounds carrots, peeled and cut into thin strips
¼ cup olive oil
¼ cup fresh sage leaves
   Kosher salt and black pepper

> Heat oven to 400° F. In a large bowl, toss the parsnips, carrots, oil, sage, 1 teaspoon salt, and ½ teaspoon pepper.

> Spread on a rimmed baking sheet and roast, stirring twice, until the vegetables are golden, 45 to 55 minutes.

TIP
If you can find only very large parsnips at the market, quarter them lengthwise and cut out the woody cores before slicing into thin strips.

Ingredients for Easy Ice Cream Cake (recipe, page 178).

desserts

Hollywood knows how to deliver a happy ending: Boy gets girl, bad guys get caught, and almost everyone gets a second chance. In the real world, ending your day—or your dinner—on a high note can be just as simple. Take your cue from the following desserts. Need a sweet that looks five-star but, really, your five-year-old could make? Try the individual apple tarts. A cool end to a cookout? Go for the ice cream layer cake. Assemble it in advance, pull it out to grand applause, and...cut.

RECIPE KEY

🕐 30 MINUTES OR LESS

♥ HEART-HEALTHY

🍲 ONE POT

🌳 VEGETARIAN

✖ NO-COOK

🧸 KID-FRIENDLY

❄ FREEZABLE

easy ice cream cake

HANDS-ON TIME: 10 MINUTES | **TOTAL TIME:** 1 HOUR, 10 MINUTES (INCLUDES CHILLING) | SERVES 6 TO 8

🍄 ✘ ♣ ❄

1 cup heavy cream

2 tablespoons confectioners' sugar

6 ice cream sandwiches (3.5 ounces each)

½ cup chocolate chips, chopped

> Line an 8½-by-4½-inch loaf pan with a piece of wax paper or parchment, allowing the paper to hang over both long sides.

> In a large bowl, beat the cream and sugar until stiff peaks form.

> In the bottom of the pan, arrange 3 of the sandwiches in a single layer, cutting them to fit as necessary. Spread with half the whipped cream. Repeat with the remaining sandwiches and whipped cream.

> Sprinkle the top of the cake with the chopped chocolate chips. Cover with plastic wrap and freeze until firm, at least 1 hour and up to 1 week.

> Holding both sides of the paper overhang, lift the cake out of the pan and transfer to a platter. Discard the paper and serve.

TIP

Upgrade this kid-friendly treat with chopped candy bars in place of the chocolate chips. Try 2 bars of Heath, Snickers, Butterfinger, or Nestlé Crunch.

roasted apple and walnut tarts

HANDS-ON TIME: 10 MINUTES | TOTAL TIME: 50 MINUTES | SERVES 4

1 8-ounce sheet frozen puff pastry, thawed

1 Cortland, McIntosh, or Empire apple, cut into ½-inch pieces

½ cup walnuts, chopped

¼ cup dark brown sugar

½ cup heavy cream

1 tablespoon confectioners' sugar

> Heat oven to 400° F.

> Cut the puff pastry into 4 squares. Line 4 cups of a muffin tin with the squares, allowing the corners to stick out.

> In a small bowl, combine the apple, walnuts, and brown sugar. Divide the mixture among the puff pastry squares and bake until the crusts are golden brown, 22 to 25 minutes. Let cool for 10 minutes before removing from the tin.

> Meanwhile, in a medium bowl, beat the cream and confectioners' sugar until soft peaks form. Serve with the tarts.

TIP
Whipped cream can be made up to 4 hours in advance. Give it a quick whisk before serving.

chocolate pots

HANDS-ON TIME: 30 MINUTES | TOTAL TIME: 2½ HOURS (INCLUDES CHILLING) | SERVES 8

⅔ cup granulated sugar

2 tablespoons cornstarch

⅛ teaspoon kosher salt

3 cups whole milk

4 large egg yolks

½ teaspoon pure vanilla extract

6 ounces bittersweet chocolate, chopped

½ teaspoon unsweetened cocoa powder

> In a medium saucepan, combine the sugar, corn-starch, and salt. Add ⅓ cup of the milk, stirring to form a smooth paste. Whisk in the egg yolks and the remaining milk.

> Cook the mixture over medium-low heat, stirring constantly with a wooden spoon or a spatula until thickened, 12 to 15 minutes (do not allow to boil). Remove from heat.

> Add the vanilla and chocolate, stirring until the chocolate is melted and the mixture is smooth. Pour into eight 4-ounce ramekins, glasses, or teacups. Refrigerate, covered, until chilled, at least 2 hours and up to 2 days. Sprinkle with the cocoa powder before serving.

TIP
Use this pudding as a creamy pie filling in a graham cracker crust. Or freeze it in ice-pop molds to make fudge pops.

boozy clementines with pound cake

HANDS-ON TIME: 15 MINUTES | TOTAL TIME: 2 HOURS, 25 MINUTES (INCLUDES CHILLING) | SERVES 8

8 clementines
1½ cups brandy
¾ cup honey
1 store-bought pound cake

> Cut away the peel and white pith from the clementines.

> In a medium saucepan, bring the brandy, honey, and 1½ cups water to a boil. Add the clementines, reduce heat, and simmer for 5 minutes. Remove from heat and let cool.

> Transfer the clementines and syrup to a serving bowl. Cover and refrigerate for at least 2 hours and up to 3 days.

> Cut the pound cake into thick slices and serve with the clementines and syrup.

TIP
To measure sticky ingredients, like honey and maple syrup, run a measuring cup or spoon under very hot water; don't let it dry. Immediately measure out the sticky ingredient. The warmth of the cup or spoon will keep it from adhering.

desserts

summer fruit pie

HANDS-ON TIME: 30 MINUTES | TOTAL TIME: 5 HOURS (INCLUDES COOLING) | SERVES 8

2½ cups flour, plus more for the work surface

1 teaspoon kosher salt

½ cup solid vegetable shortening (such as Crisco), chilled

½ cup (1 stick) plus 4 tablespoons unsalted butter, chilled and cut into small cubes

1 large egg

1 tablespoon white vinegar

6 ripe peaches, each cut into 8 wedges

1 pint strawberries, halved

¼ cup instant tapioca

3 tablespoons fresh lemon juice

½ cup plus 2 tablespoons granulated sugar

> In a food processor, combine the flour, salt, shortening, and ½ cup of the butter until the mixture forms pea-size crumbs. Break the egg into a measuring cup and beat lightly; add the vinegar and enough cold water to measure ½ cup. Slowly add the egg mixture to the flour mixture, pulsing until a soft dough forms.

> Divide the dough in half. Shape each half into a flat disk. Wrap in plastic and refrigerate for at least 1 hour.

> On a lightly floured surface, roll out 1 disk into a 14-inch circle. Place in a 2-inch-deep 9-inch pie plate.

> In a medium bowl, gently toss the peaches, strawberries, tapioca, lemon juice, and ½ cup of the sugar. Spoon the fruit mixture into the pie plate and dot with the remaining 4 tablespoons of butter; refrigerate.

> Roll out the second disk of dough into a 14-inch circle. Drape it over the pie and trim the edge to a ½-inch overhang. Fold under, pressing to seal. Crimp the edge, if desired. Refrigerate for at least 30 minutes.

> Heat oven to 425° F. Lightly brush the top crust with cold water and sprinkle with the remaining sugar. Cut several slashes into the top crust. Bake until golden, 18 to 22 minutes. Reduce heat to 375° F and continue to bake until the juices bubble, 30 to 40 minutes more.

> Transfer to a rack and cool for 2 hours before serving.

croissant and chocolate bread pudding

HANDS-ON TIME: 10 MINUTES | TOTAL TIME: 50 MINUTES | SERVES 8

Unsalted butter for the baking dish
6 large egg yolks
2 cups whole milk
1 cup heavy cream
1 cup granulated sugar
1 teaspoon pure vanilla extract
½ teaspoon kosher salt
½ teaspoon ground nutmeg
6 croissants, cut into 1-inch pieces
(about 1 pound)
4 ounces bittersweet chocolate,
cut into chunks

> Heat oven to 375° F. Butter an 8-inch square baking dish or some other shallow 2-quart baking dish.

> In a large bowl, whisk together the egg yolks, milk, cream, sugar, vanilla, salt, and nutmeg. Add the croissants and chocolate and mix to combine.

> Transfer the mixture to the prepared baking dish. Bake until set and a knife inserted in the center comes out clean, 30 to 40 minutes. Serve warm or at room temperature.

TIP
For a grown-up dessert
or a hair-of-the-dog
brunch, whisk a couple of
tablespoons of amaretto,
Kahlúa, or brandy into the
egg mixture.

berry shortcakes

HANDS-ON TIME: 10 MINUTES | TOTAL TIME: 20 MINUTES | SERVES 8

2 pounds berries (such as raspberries, blueberries, or sliced strawberries)

⅓ cup plus 2 tablespoons granulated sugar

1 cup heavy cream

8 biscuits, store-bought or made from a mix

> In a large bowl, toss the berries and ⅓ cup of the sugar. Let sit for at least 15 minutes (and up to 4 hours, refrigerated).

> In a medium bowl, beat the cream and the remaining 2 tablespoons of sugar until soft peaks form.

> Split the biscuits in half. Spoon the berries and whipped cream on the bottom halves and sandwich with the tops.

apricot-coconut cake

HANDS-ON TIME: 30 MINUTES | TOTAL TIME: 3½ HOURS (INCLUDES COOLING) | SERVES 8

1 cup shredded sweetened coconut

¾ cup (1½ sticks) unsalted butter, at room temperature, plus more for the pans

3 cups all-purpose flour

2 teaspoons baking powder

½ teaspoon kosher salt

1½ cups granulated sugar

4 large eggs

1 teaspoon pure vanilla extract

1¼ cups apricot preserves

1 cup whole milk

1 cup heavy cream

¼ cup sour cream

2 tablespoons confectioners' sugar

> Heat oven to 350° F. Toast the coconut on a baking sheet, tossing occasionally, until golden, 10 to 12 minutes. Butter two 8-inch round cake pans. In a large bowl, whisk together the flour, baking powder, and salt.

> Using an electric mixer, beat the butter and granulated sugar until fluffy. Beat in the eggs one at a time, then the vanilla and ¾ cup of the preserves. Alternately add the flour mixture and milk, mixing just until incorporated.

> Divide the batter between the pans and bake until a toothpick inserted in the centers comes out clean, 40 to 45 minutes. Remove the cakes from the pans and let cool completely on racks.

> Using an electric mixer, beat the heavy cream, sour cream, and confectioners' sugar until stiff peaks form. Spread the remaining ½ cup of preserves on top of one of the cakes; sandwich with the other. Frost with the cream mixture and press the coconut onto the sides.

TIP
The cakes can be baked, wrapped tightly, and stored (unfrosted) at room temperature for up to 2 days. Frost up to 4 hours before serving.

menu suggestions

Since a recipe (usually) does not a meal make, here are winning combinations for all sorts of occasions.

WEEKEND BRUNCH
- sausage with warm tomatoes and hash browns
- basic quiche
- croissant and chocolate bread pudding

SHOWER LUNCHEON
- Parmesan twists
- gazpacho
- salmon and fennel with roasted-lemon vinaigrette
- boozy clementines with pound cake

ALL-AMERICAN BARBECUE
- dry-rubbed baby-back ribs
- parsleyed corn on the cob
- coleslaw with caraway and raisins
- berry shortcakes

BACKYARD PICNIC
- sweet and tangy wings with butter lettuce salad
- new potato and watercress salad
- summer fruit pie

GAME-DAY GATHERING
- fancy pigs in a blanket
- provolone and roasted red pepper crisps
- southwestern beef chili with corn
- easy ice cream cake

WINTER LUNCH
- butternut squash soup
- potato and leek flat bread with greens
- roasted apple and walnut tarts

COOKING FOR A CROWD
- Parmesan twists
- Greek salad with basil dressing
- lasagna-style baked ziti
- berry shortcakes

FANCY DINNER PARTY
- pears with blue cheese and prosciutto
- rosemary pecans
- chicken with creamy spinach and shallots
- Parmesan roasted potatoes
- boozy clementines with pound cake

COMFORT-FOOD DINNER
- turkey meat loaf with mashed potatoes
- roasted parsnips and carrots with sage
- chocolate pots

WEEKNIGHT GUESTS
- goat cheese bruschetta
- lamb chops with tomatoes and olives
- roasted apple and walnut tarts

SUNDAY SUPPER
- roast pork and asparagus with mustard vinaigrette
- sautéed tomatoes and shallots
- Cheddar and scallion grits
- summer fruit pie

VEGETARIAN DINNER
- provolone and roasted red pepper crisps
- sweet potato risotto
- broiled asparagus

ITALIAN DINNER
- pears with blue cheese and prosciutto
- spinach salad with warm onions and crispy salami
- linguine with tomato sauce
- sautéed zucchini

INDIAN DINNER
- easy samosas
- curried rice with shrimp
- apricot-coconut cake

LAST-MINUTE MEAL
- angel hair with spicy shrimp
- sautéed tomatoes and shallots

CHILD'S BIRTHDAY
- fancy pigs in a blanket
- macaroni and cheese
- easy ice cream cake

MILESTONE BIRTHDAY
- beef cocktail sandwiches with parsley butter
- smoked salmon and horseradish cream with potato chips
- baked cod and chorizo
- apricot-coconut cake

10 recipes for a great dinner party
- crispy breaded shrimp with cannellini beans
- deep-dish polenta pizza
- fisherman's soup
- grilled mahimahi with grapefruit, avocado, and watercress
- poached scallops with leeks and carrots
- roast pork and asparagus with mustard vinaigrette
- salmon and fennel with roasted-lemon vinaigrette
- spiced lamb chops and smashed peas
- steak with cauliflower and crunchy bread crumbs
- tortellini with eggplant and peppers

charts

A little technical support for your adventures in the kitchen.

Meat Cooking Temperatures

The safest, most accurate way to figure out when your poultry and other meats are perfectly cooked is by checking the internal temperature with an instant-read thermometer. Follow the guidelines on this chart and your meat should be tender and juicy.

POULTRY

Boneless chicken breasts . . . . 160° to 165° F*

Chicken and turkey cutlets . . . . 160° to 165° F

Chicken wings . . . . 165° F

Bone-in chicken breasts, thighs,
and drumsticks . . . . 160° to 165° F

BEEF

Steaks ¹/₂ to 1 inch thick
(such as flank or skirt) . . . . 130° to 145° F

Steaks 1 to 1¹/₂ inches thick
(such as strip or London broil) . . . . 130° to 145° F

Hamburgers 1 inch thick . . . . 155° to 160° F

PORK

Tenderloin . . . . 150° to 160° F

Chops ³/₄ to 1 inch thick . . . . 150° to 160° F

Baby-back ribs . . . . 150° to 160° F

LAMB

Chops ¹/₂ to 1 inch thick . . . . 130° to 145° F

Chops 1 to 1¹/₂ inches thick . . . . 130° to 145° F

Butterflied boneless leg
(1 to 1¹/₂ inches thick) . . . . 130° to 145° F

Where temperatures appear as a range, the higher figure is the U.S. Department of Agriculture's recommendation for maximum food safety. The lower temperature, considered safe by many food experts, is the Real Simple test kitchen's preference.

Baking-Pan Substitutions

When you don't have the pan that a recipe calls for, often others can do just as well. (Shallower pans may require shorter baking times.)

PAN SIZE	CAPACITY	SUBSTITUTIONS
9-by-2-inch round	8 cups	8-by-8-by-2-inch square 11-by-7-by-2-inch rectangle 2 12-cupcake tins
8-by-8-by-2-inch square	8³/₄ cups	9-by-2-inch round 2 8¹/₂-by-4¹/₂-by-2¹/₂-inch loaf pans 2 12-cupcake tins
9-by-13-by-2-inch rectangle	16 cups	2 9-by-2-inch rounds 2 8-by-8-by-2-inch squares 4 12-cupcake tins
8¹/₂-by-4¹/₂-by-2¹/₂-inch loaf	6 cups	9-by-2-inch round 8-by-8-by-2-inch square 12-cupcake tin 11-by-7-by-2-inch rectangle
12-cupcake tin	6 cups	9-by-2-inch round 8-by-8-by-2-inch square 11-by-7-by-2-inch rectangle
11-by-7-by-2-inch rectangle	8 cups	9-by-2-inch round 8-by-8-by-2-inch square 2 12-cupcake tins

Measuring Cheat Sheet

3 teaspoons: 1 tablespoon	4 cups: 1 quart
4 tablespoons: ¹/₄ cup	2 pints: 1 quart
16 tablespoons: 1 cup	4 quarts: 1 gallon
2 cups: 1 pint	1 pound: 16 ounces

nutritional information

A by-the-numbers guide to what's in every recipe.

RECIPE KEY

🕐 30 MINUTES OR LESS

♥ HEART-HEALTHY*

🍲 ONE POT

🍄 VEGETARIAN

✖ NO-COOK

👪 KID-FRIENDLY

❄ FREEZABLE

*The designation of a recipe as heart-healthy is based on the number of calories and the amount of total fat and saturated fat, sodium, and cholesterol. The specific criteria vary by the category of the dish (starchy side dish, vegetarian entrée, and so on).

index

Looking for a great soup or a way to use those apples from the farmers' market? Find it here.

credits

REAL SIMPLE

Managing Editor Kristin van Ogtrop
Creative Director Janet Froelich
Executive Editor Sarah Humphreys
Deputy Managing Editor Jacklyn Monk
Design Director Ellene Wundrok
Deputy Editor Rachel Hardage
Food Director Allison Lewis Clapp
Senior Editor Lygeia Grace
Food Stylist Sara Quessenberry
Associate Food Editor Kate Merker
Art Director Ronald Sequeira
Photo Director Casey Tierney
Copy Chief Nancy Negovetich
Copy Editor Janet Kim
Research Chief Westry Green
Research Editor Maya Kukes
Associate Research Editor Claudia Bloom
Researchers Stephanie Abramson, Carlos Greer,
Allegra Muzzillo
Editorial Production Director Jeff Nesmith
Assistant Editorial Production Manager Albert Young
Imaging Director Richard Prue
Imaging Manager Claudio Muller

President, Lifestyle Group Steve Sachs
Publisher Kevin White
Vice President, Consumer Marketing Carrie Goldin
Executive Director of Brand Development & Strategy
M. Gary Ryan
Advertising Director Melissa Gasper
Director, Public Relations Amanda Potters
Marketing Director Sarah Kate Ellis

TIME INC. HOME ENTERTAINMENT

Publisher Richard Fraiman
General Manager Steven Sandonato
Executive Director, Marketing Services Carol Pittard
Director, Retail & Special Sales Tom Mifsud
Director, New Product Development Peter Harper
Assistant Director, Bookazine Marketing Laura Adam
Assistant Publishing Director, Brand Marketing
Joy Butts
Associate Counsel Helen Wan
Marketing Manager Victoria Alfonso
Design & Prepress Manager Anne-Michelle Gallero
Book Production Manager Susan Chodakiewicz

SPECIAL THANKS

Katrine Ames, Pam Anderson, Christine Austin,
Frances Boswell, Stephana Bottom, Terri Bowles,
Glenn Buonocore, Elizabeth Burkhalter, Jim Childs,
Kay Chun, Rose Cirrincione, Lauren Epstein,
Jacqueline Fitzgerald, Lindsay Funston, Susan
Getzendanner, Candice Gianetti, Elizabeth
Grover, Caroline Gottesman, Katherine Green-
wald, Pamela Grossman, Jenni Hakensen, Lauren
Hall, Kai Jacob, Jennifer Jacobs, Suzanne Janso,
Brynn Joyce, Jane Kirby, Emma Knowles, Mona Li,
Paul and Lou Maki, Robert Marasco, Cyd Raftus
McDowell, Amy Migliaccio, Megan Moore,
Melinda Page, Amy Palanjian, Elizabeth Passarella,
James Peterson, Kaitlyn Pirie, Brooke Reger, Dave
Rozzelle, Ilene Schreider, Virginia Sole-Smith,
Katy Sparks, Susie Theodorou, Adriana Tierno,
Suzy Verrier, Alex Voznesenskiy, Sydney Webber

Copyright © 2009
by Time Inc. Home Entertainment
Published by Real Simple Books,
a trademark of Time Inc.
1271 Avenue of the Americas
New York, NY 10020

First printing October 2009

ISBN 13: 978-1-60320-102-5
ISBN 10: 1-60320-102-5
Library of Congress Number: 2009928257

We welcome your comments and suggestions
about Real Simple Books. Please e-mail us at
books@realsimple.com, or write us at:
Real Simple Books
1271 Avenue of the Americas
New York, NY 10020

PRINTED IN CHINA

PHOTO CREDITS

Antonis Achilleos: pages 12, 69, 85, 204
Pam Anderson: page 50
Burcu Avsar: page 141
Quentin Bacon: pages 17, 138, 171
James Baigrie: pages 167, 173
Christopher Baker: page 166
Justin Bernhaut: page 174
Hallie Burton: pages 98, 114
Lisa Cohen: page 101
Beatriz DaCosta: pages 11, 13, 15, 77, 125, 165,
180, 183
Formula Z/S: page 4
Dana Gallagher: pages 12, 69, 85, back cover
Thayer Allyson Gowdy: page 194
Lisa Hubbard: pages 61, 86, 168
Ditte Isager: pages 72–73
Frances Janisch: page 110
Kan Kanbayashi: pages 129, 145
Kana Okada: front cover, pages 38, 54, 146, 169
John Kernick: pages 150, 157, 191
David Loftus: page 90
Maura McEvoy: page 197
Miha Matei: pages 57, 134
William Meppem: page 126
James Merrell: pages 78, 102
Ngoc Minh Ngo: pages 49, 74, 81, 89, 93, 154
Marcus Nilsson: pages 45, 66, 70, 94, 137, 142,
158, 176, 179
Michael Paul: page 41
Con Poulos: pages 21, 26, 33, 37, 162, 164,
175, 188, 192
Maria Robledo: page 65
Hector Sanchez: pages 82, 122, 133, 153
Sang An: pages 18, 29, 34, 113, 198
Time Inc. Digital Studio: pages 160–161
Petrina Tinslay: pages 25, 105, 149, 170, 172
Mikkel Vang: pages 9, 14
Anna Williams: pages 8, 10, 22, 30, 42, 58, 97,
106, 109, 120, 121, 184

If you would like to order any of our hardcover Collector's edition books, please call us at
1-800-327-6388 (Monday through Friday, 7 A.M. to 8 P.M., or Saturday, 7 A.M. to 6 P.M., central time).